THIS WE BELIEVE

BY

JAMES H. WALTNER

ILLUSTRATED BY

ANNIE VALLOTTON

FAITH AND LIFE PRESS
NEWTON, KANSAS

Preface

One frequently hears it said, "It doesn't matter what you believe; it's what you do that counts." The underlying assumption seems to be that as long as people are running around doing something, somehow everything will turn out all right. Will it? Are we going somewhere or are we merely running around in circles?

Of course, action speaks louder than words. Right action is terribly important. But we must not forget that what we *do* is dependent upon what we *believe*. Belief determines action. G. K. Chesterton once said that it is more important for a landlady to know what her tenant believes than to know his bank account.

What is belief? Is it the same as having an opinion? Hardly. Opinions dominate most of our small talk and some that isn't small. Beliefs, as we think of them in this book, mean our basic convictions about the important questions of life. Beliefs deal with the meanings of life. Who am I? What is my place in life, and what is the meaning of life? What is God like? Who is Christ? What is the church? What about evil, suffering, and tyranny?

The title of this book refers to the body of Christian teaching which Christians hold to be true. These beliefs, if we accept them, become a launching pad for our actions. There are many kinds of beliefs in the world today. One result of studying this book will be that you must decide what *you* believe.

WILLARD CLAASSEN

Acknowledgments

This study guide represents the work of many people. Overall guidance and planning was provided by a curriculum committee consisting of Paul R. Shelly, chairman; Jacob Enz; Mrs. Leland Harder; Helmut Harder; Lyman Hofstetter; Arthur Isaak; and H. T. Klassen. During the year in which the project was in progress, two new members were added to the curriculum group: Mrs. Delton Franz and James Mohr. All of these persons had opportunity to review the outlines and evaluate the manuscript, thus providing many helpful suggestions to the writer and editor. This group decided what shape this study guide should take.

The outlines for *This We Believe* were formulated by Paul R. Shelly, Milton Harder, Arthur Isaak, H. T. Klassen, Heinz Janzen, and Willard Claassen. They are based on the earlier publication, *My Christian Faith*.

During the period of writing, James H. Waltner was pastor of a congregation near Newton, Kansas. He had opportunity to test many of the ideas expressed in this book with fellow pastors and with his own young people.

Deliberate effort was made to acknowledge all sources either in the text or footnotes appearing at the end of chapters.

WILLARD CLAASSEN

Contents

Chapter 1

Life's Top Priority

For whoever would draw near to God must believe that he exists. . . .   Hebrews 11:6

Who am I?

This fellow is thinking. It's obvious he's not making a sound. Yet he is crying out. What do you hear him say?

Is it, "Lord, help my unbelief!"?

Or could it be, "Lord, I have already felt some stirrings of your transforming power within me; give me the further help that I must have if Christian faith is to be mine!"?

WHO AM I?

Tomorrow is Jean's sixteenth birthday. Sixteen at last! Sixteen! Jean feels like skipping and shouting! A sudden surge of freedom and power races through her.

The mirror reassures her —no child anymore am I! A junior in high school.

1

Next year a senior—and then college! Career? Marriage?

Why does it take so long to grow up? Why does time move so slowly? And how can Mother say it was just yesterday that I was her little baby?

Was I ever really like baby Sue—fussing and crying and clamoring for attention until someone picked me up, or until I fell asleep? Or like five-year-old Billy? He gets the attention all right! Teasing, asking questions, pouting. He acts as if he's the most important person in the world!

I can remember when I started school, Jean thought. Mrs. Adams was so nice . . . and how I tried to please her . . . and the fun I had playing with the other children!

Then there was Karen, who joined our class in the sixth grade. She was born in Tokyo, where she lived until her parents moved here. So we studied about Japan and other countries and people who are different. Mr. Roberts told us that the chance of our being born in America was about one in twenty. One-fourth of the world's babies are born in China. Mr. Roberts also said something about only one chance in four of being born into a home that is Christian.

Or to think that people lived on earth for hundreds and thousands of years. People are born, they live, they die. Mr. Smith asked us the other day if we thought there are people on other planets . . . Mars maybe? What about other worlds like ours?

Jean stared into the mirror. Sixteen! Who am I really? Why am I here? Where am I going? What is life all about?

These are questions of *existence*. They always bring us to the question of *the ultimate*. Is there some ultimate purpose for my being here? Some divine power? Or am I here by chance, and for myself alone?

In answer to Jean's and our questions about life, the Christian faith makes some claims.

WHAT'S IT ALL ABOUT?

Who am I? Why am I here? One of the clearest statements of God's purpose for the world—and for people—is found in Ephe-

2

sians 1:9-12. The writer contends that God has *a plan . . . to unite all things in him* (v. 10). God's blueprint for us is *to live for the praise of his glory* (v. 12). Our purpose is to proclaim God is here and at work!

The Gospel of Mark, earliest summary account of Jesus' life and work, introduces Jesus, *Jesus came into Galilee, preaching the Gospel of God, and saying, "The time is fulfilled, and the kingdom of God is at hand; repent, and believe in the gospel"* (Mk. 1:14, 15). The good news of "the kingdom" that Jesus spoke about was the reign of God. Jesus was proclaiming that God rules over the world and the people He has made! We begin to enter "the kingdom" when we discover who we really are— small, helpless, dependent creatures in our selfish rebellion. "The kingdom" becomes effective in our lives as we respond to God by acknowledging Him as the source and center of life. That this is possible at all is because God shows himself to us in the person of Jesus Christ.

Another statement of the Christian claim may be found in Matthew 6:24, 25, 31-34. Jesus says, *No one can serve two masters. . . . But seek first his kingdom and his righteousness, and all these things shall be yours as well* (vv. 24, 33). If God is the source of life, and He has a basic purpose for us, what about the needs we think we have? Aren't food, clothing, and shelter important? Ought we not be concerned about these things for ourselves? When does worry and fretfulness over things such as food, clothing, and shelter become a denial of God?

It is the claim of Christian faith that God exists, and that He has an aim and purpose for each human life. That God exists means that the world is not the result of chance. All begins with God—and not with me! He is host; I am guest. He has made me, and found me again in Christ. In finding me, He wants me to discover myself as His child. As I become aware of the need of some purpose beyond myself, as I see how Jesus Christ came to show me God's love, as I accept this love, I find my true purpose. The prayer of an early Christian says it this way, "O Lord, we are restless, until we find our rest in thee."

REACTING TO THIS CLAIM

Question: What do you think about the claim of the Christian faith that God is central in the world?

Bill: "Wait a minute. Here we are with all sorts of pressing thoughts and concerns—school, job, or college? Government service—and you talk to us about God. We're sort of puzzled. We're not even sure we know what you mean."

Frank: "Sure, I believe in God. I think it's a good thing. I want to have somebody I can pray to when I'm in trouble. Makes you a better person, too."

Pat: "What's the difference? I mean, I don't see that it matters much whether you believe in God or not. From what I see most people are about the same. Nobody really pays much attention to church and things like that anymore."

What is your own response to the claim of the Christian faith that God is central in life?

What are some of the goals, purposes, and aims that people have? What are the most important goals of the young people with whom you go to school? Would your aims be the same? How do these affect your response to the Christian claim that God is central?

What does John 1:9-12 say to you about the reaction of the world to the Christian claim about God? What does it say to you—about yourself?

THE PLACE OF DOUBT IN FAITH

"I'm stumped when I ponder the clods who are firm in
      Their faith in a Power up yonder—
  But I'm stumped a lot more when I try to determine
      Where I got the power to ponder."[1]

Have you ever wondered about that? Where do we get the right —even the idea, to ask questions about ourselves, about the world, and about God? Should we ask these questions?

Doubt is often searching—an attempt to exchange a second-hand religion for firsthand, personal faith. Faith is growth. We sometimes step out in faith with doubt unresolved. Perhaps this can help us understand that statement of the man in Mark 9:24: *I believe; help my unbelief!*

In our study of Christian faith, as we ask, "How do I put God first?" we will be working also with the questions and the doubts that are ours. We will seek to strengthen the faith already ours.

A LOOK AHEAD

The study of Christian faith is divided into twenty-eight sessions, organized under the following six units:

    I. God and His World
    II. Man and Sin
    III. Jesus Christ and Salvation
    IV. The Church and Its Task
    V. The Life of Discipleship
    VI. The Christian Hope

The Bible will be our text; Christians believe God guided persons to write it. We will use this book as a study guide. Each chapter will include questions about Christian beliefs and point to key Bible passages for study. You will also find questions with several possible answers to which you will be asked to respond.

No A's, B's, or C's are given in a course like this. Much more than a "grade" is at stake, a life on the beam, or a life lost. How deep you will probe, and how helpful this study guide becomes will depend on you.

WORDS AND DEFINITIONS

Words are tools we need in research, in understanding, and in expression. In this study, we will meet some new words and some new definitions of old words. Let's begin with two:

*Anthropo*s (man) + *logos* (word) = anthropology (word about man)

Theos (God) + *logos* (word) = theology (word about God)

Anthropology is study about man. Theology is study about God. If God is the central fact about the universe, then we are not. And that discovery can make all the difference as to how you and I will live our lives.

WHAT CAN HAPPEN TO YOU IN THIS STUDY?

1. You may discover that beliefs are important after all, that the attitude, "It doesn't matter what you believe, just so you believe something," is just not adequate.

2. You may discover that God is more than an idea, more than "an impersonal someone-out-there." You may find that God is concerned about and loves *you*.

3. You may find yourself swept up in the exciting drama of life, and realize you are under orders from God for a crucial mission.

4. To make a serious study of the Christian beliefs could be your life's most exciting frontier! It can happen!

FOR YOU TO DO

What do you find yourself saying to God as you begin this study of Christian belief? Think this out prayerfully and write it below as your prayer.

1. Julian Brown, "Confession," *The Mennonite,* 80:35 (September 28, 1965), p. 600.

Chapter 2

How Can I Know God?

> *O Lord, thou hast searched*
> *me and known me!*
> *Thou knowest when I sit down and*
> *when I rise up;*
> *thou discernest my thoughts from afar. . . .*
> *Whither shall I go from thy Spirit?*
> *Or whither shall I flee from thy presence?*
> Psalm 139:1, 2, 7

THE INESCAPABLE GOD

The Indian ascetic, who lies on a bed of spikes to punish his body so that his soul may be purified, is seeking God. The Hindu philosopher will spend hours in strictly disciplined meditation to arrive at the knowledge of "Brahman," the soul of the universe. The Muslim recites his creed and prays five times a day with his face toward Mecca. The devout Jew who faithfully reads and seeks to obey the Law is seeking to know God.

How can I know God? How can I know God exists? How can I know what God is like? How can I know that God knows me? These questions have been asked—sometimes out of fear and earnest searching—sometimes out of anger and rebellion.

Psalm 139 was written by a man who was convinced that God is knowable. He discovered that everywhere he went, God was there. God could not be evaded.

The unique claim of the Christian faith about God is not only that God is "knowable," but that it is *God who makes himself known to us.* Long before we even consciously reach out to Him, God takes the initiative in revealing himself. How does He show himself?

7

GOD'S WAY OF GETTING THROUGH TO US

Here are several ways by which God makes himself known to us. These are not God, nor even proofs of God, but they are pointers to God. Test yourself to see whether God has been able to get through to you by any of these ways.

1. *Nature*

Read Psalm 19:1-4.

Charles M. Beebe said of his visits to Theodore Roosevelt: "After an evening of talk, perhaps about the fringes of knowledge, . . . we would go out on the lawn, where we took turns at an amusing little astronomical rite. We searched until we found, with or without glasses, the faint, heavenly spot of light-mist beyond the lower left-hand corner of the Great Square of Pegasus, when one or the other of us would then recite:

That is the Spiral Galaxy in Andromeda.

It is as large as our Milky Way.

It is one of a hundred million galaxies.

It is 750,000 light-years away.

It consists of one hundred billion suns,
    each larger than our sun.

After an interval Colonel Roosevelt would grin at me and say: "Now I think we are small enough! Let's go to bed."[2]

Who has not caught a glimpse of the immense majesty, the beauty in the world of nature?

The power and regularity of the sun and planets and constellations of stars.

The freshness of the morning, or the wondrous colors of the evening sky.

The rugged grandeur of the Rockies.

The forests of green, fields of golden grain, a blanket of white snow.

The sense of mystery in the many-colored wings of a butterfly, or the intricate organization of a colony of bees?

Paul wrote to the Romans:

For what can be known about God is plain to them, because

God has shown it to them. Ever since the creation of the world his invisible nature, namely, his eternal power and deity, has been clearly perceived in the things that have been made (Rom. 1:19, 20).

This world around us can *point* to God. But it does not necessarily *lead* to God. For there is also disorder, ugliness, and death, and a host of apparently meaningless things in this same world.

Besides that, Paul says in Romans 1:19-25 that the people who ought to be able to see God in the world He has made, often do not. Through the sin of our pride we begin to worship the created things rather than the Creator. Gold and silver, land, steel, concrete, machines, and governments become our gods. And so, says Paul, men become *fools . . . exchanging the splendour of immortal God for an image shaped like mortal man* (Rom. 1:23 NEB).

God's relevation of himself in the world of nature while helpful is not enough.

2. *The Conscience*

Gwen sailed through the history exam with flying colors. Her mark is tops in the class. But in her heart she feels uneasy. For she knows she has been untrue to her classmates, to her teacher, and to herself. She cheated on that exam. No one else knows it, but Gwen knows it.

The psalmist long ago confessed, *Behold, thou desirest truth in the inward being* (51:6).

Our feelings of guilt may be God's way of speaking to us. Read the story of Cain in Genesis 4:1-15. We are told that Cain was angry with God because the offerings of his brother Abel appeared more acceptable to God. Cain accuses God for his irritation.

Because he knows Cain's feet are on slippery ground, God tries to warn him, and help him find a clearer insight into himself. *"Why are you angry? . . . sin is couching at the door; its desire is for you, but you must master it"* (v. 7).

But Cain does not heed the voice, and in rebellion slays his brother. Instead of losing patience, God continues His effort to get through to Cain. *"Where is Abel your brother?"* . . . *"What have you done?"* God asks. The questions invite Cain to turn within himself and to acknowledge his guilt so that he may find forgiving grace.

God speaks to us—even in our guilt—even in our feelings of wrongdoing. He is trying to awaken us to repentance and grace through our consciousness of guilt.

But conscience does not always lead us to God. Conscience can become blunted so that we become deaf to God's voice. Or we may turn in upon ourselves and feel so guilty and unworthy and be in such terror of God that we think there is no use trying anymore. So God shows himself also in other ways.

3. *Our Experience*

"I was on my way to a track meet," said Vince Gibson, football coach at Kansas State University, "unaware that what was to happen in the next few moments would become one of the most frightening, yet spiritually rewarding experiences in my life.

"As I drove away from my office and neared the bottom of the hill close to the Tennessee River, I put my foot on the brake. Carelessly it slipped onto the accelerator and shot my car ahead. Quickly I put my foot on the brake, but it was too late. A man driving from the opposite direction thought I was coming onto his side so he swerved to his left, crossed the street, jumped a guard rail and plunged down a 20-foot embankment into the Tennessee River."

In the next minutes Vince Gibson dived into the river to help the driver who rolled out of his car as it sank beneath the surface. With the help of another swimmer, he brought the unconscious man to shore. The artificial respiration they administered revived him.

"All of a sudden it hit me that God saved that man's life. What would have happened if the door had not opened and the body had sunk into the 30-foot water? It took the divers four hours to find the car. What would have happened if when I got to the man he would have fought me and panicked, because I am not that good a swimmer? . . . I know that on the banks of the Tennessee River, God was with me. He saved my life and his."[3]

Have you ever felt God come close to you? Moses did as he struggled with the choice of vocation (Ex. 3:1-13). Isaiah did during worship at a time of national crisis (Is. 6:1-13). Saul of Tarsus did in his stubborn rebellion against Christ (Acts 9:1-19).

And for nineteen centuries now, since the time Jesus of Nazareth lived upon the earth, men and women of all ages have felt that God has come close to them, in their work, in the joy of living, in the frightening experiences of life, and in moments of inward searching.

A high school sophomore girl writes about the time she felt God was speaking to her, "It was shortly after my father's death that I first felt God speaking to me. I had finished the dishes and was sitting on the porch feeling sorry for myself when I started thinking about things that hadn't really mattered much to me before. Who was God? What was it that made people willing to die for Him, a person they had never seen before? The questions went on and on and somehow they were being answered. Then suddenly I knew that I, too, wanted to be a Christian."

Can we disregard all of this as imagination? Or are there times when we sense our relationship to someone much greater than ourselves?

But even our experiences, and those of others, are not sufficient. God chose yet another way, a very special way, to make himself known, and to help us understand our experience.

4. *The Bible*

The Bible expresses the conviction that God has been showing himself through the great events that took place in the life of His people. The history of Israel is the history of what God has done and said, and how Israel responded.

But the Bible goes beyond portraying the God of history. Here also, we see how God shows himself to us through persons. The theme of the Bible is God's love for man, love so great that God sent Jesus into the world to suffer, and even to die for man. It is through the Bible and our knowledge of Jesus Christ, that we come to know the presence and work of God most clearly. Here we find the God who is concerned about individuals. Here is a record of how God revealed himself to Abraham, David, Peter, and others. Here, too, is the response of these men and women to God.

And here is the story of the Christian church—how God called the church into being, and His purpose for us through the church.

How God speaks to us through the Bible, and how the Bible can become a guide for Christian faith is the topic of the next session.

A WORD TO REMEMBER

Revelation. God discloses himself to us. We do not happen to discover God on our own. He makes himself and His will known to us.

WHAT DO YOU THINK

1. Has God been able to get through to you by any of the ways mentioned? What other ways might God be using?

2. What are some of the barriers we deliberately or unknowingly erect to shut God out?

3. Discuss the statement, "People do not find God in trees and mountains—unless they find Him in Christ." Do you agree or disagree? Why? Here it may be helpful to read John 1:14-18.

4. We live in a time when people demand scientific proofs. Can all truth be "proved" by scientific methods?

5. Is our knowledge of God something we can be certain about?

6. Think of one specific experience when God may have been speaking to you. Does His presence in that experience seem clearer now than it did at that time?

PRAYERS

"O Thou who knowest me so utterly, help me to know Thee a little" (Unknown).

"Lord, be Thou within me, to strengthen me; without me, to

keep me; above me, to protect me; beneath me, to uphold me; before me, to direct me; behind me, to keep me from straying; round about me, to defend me. Blessed be Thou, our Father, for ever and ever" (Lancelot Andrews d. 1626, Bishop of Winchester).

2. Charles M. Beebe, *The Book of Naturalists* (New York: Alfred A. Knopf, 1944), p. 234.

3. *The Christian Athlete,* 9:7 (September 1965), pp. 3, 4.

Chapter 3

The Bible --
God's Own Textbook

But as for you, continue in what you have learned and have firmly believed, knowing from whom you learned it and how from childhood you have been acquainted with the sacred writings which are able to instruct you for salvation through faith in Christ Jesus. All scripture is inspired by God and profitable for teaching, for reproof, for correction, and for training in righteousness, that the man of God may be complete, equipped for every good work.

2 Timothy 3:14-17

THE BIBLE—AND FIRE!

Dateline: July 6, 1415. An angry mob milled around in a field outside a south German village. The center of attention was a thin, unassuming man, bound by cords to a wooden post. On his head was a paper hat with the word "heretic."

A cardinal of the church, in flowing red robes, approached the man at the stake asking him to recant. He replied, "God is my witness that the evidence against me is false. In the truth of the gospel I have written, taught, and preached; today I will gladly die. I must obey the Scriptures." And as John Huss sang out in a loud voice, the smoke and flames began to blow in his face.

In 1428 the bones of another man, dead for forty years, were dug up and burned. The crime: making it possible for people to read the Scriptures in their own language. John Wycliffe, a minister in England, believed that "No man was so rude a scholar but that he might learn the words of a Gospel." Out of this conviction came the first partial translation of the Bible into English. But Wycliffe's reward was to have his bones dug up and burned.

Again in 1536, still another man was burned at the stake. This time it was William Tyndale who translated almost the whole Bible into English. Tyndale's work laid the basis for the English translations of the Bible we use today.

Why did these men do it? What made Huss and Wycliffe and Tyndale risk their lives that other people could read the Bible? What is there about this book that makes some persons today devote their whole lifetime to studying, translating, distributing, and teaching it?

OUR PROBLEM

Student (with rising voice): "But why should I bother to read the Bible anyway? Tell me why I should worry about the problems they had in 700 B.C.! I've got my own problems to think about—here and now!"

Why do I have to read the Bible anyway? Good question! And it says something about the problems we have with the Bible. Can we identify them?

1. *The Bible is a thick book,* over a thousand pages of small print. We prefer shorter books. And to say that the Bible is a collection of shorter books doesn't help much. Who wants to carry a whole library around?

2. *The books of the Bible come out of a different time and culture.* It is difficult enough to think oneself into the country and time and customs in which Jesus lived nearly two thousand years ago, but the Old Testament is even older than that. To discover that the books of the Bible were written at different periods of time, over a span of one thousand years, in a variety of circumstances, doesn't make it easier. How are we to know, for example, that when Psalm 23 was written, anointing the head with oil referred to a way of being hospitable to a guest, as we offer someone a cup of coffee or tea nowadays? Even the way people thought and spoke about things was different. We

15

might say, "It rained this afternoon." The oriental people, who were inclined to interpret all of life in religious terms, would have said, "The Lord sent rain upon the earth."

3. *The Bible contains many stories and incidents called signs and miracles.* There is a story about the sun standing still for a day (Josh. 10:12-15); an axe head floating on the water (2 Kings 6:5, 6); the crowd of five thousand fed with a boy's lunch of five loaves and two fish (Jn. 6:5-14); and the raising to life of a man who had been dead for four days (Jn. 11:38-44). What can we make of these and all the other stories that somehow don't seem to fit the laws about life we have come to know?

4. *We so often get the Bible piecemeal.* We pick up a story here, a sentence there, without any sense of the major theme, and the sweep of the whole story. The early Hebrew Old Testament and Greek New Testament manuscripts were written without word and sentence divisions. BUTSINCETHISISSODIFFICULT TOREAD, Bible scholars later added the punctuation. The chapter divisions were made in 1228, and the verse divisions in 1551. A French printer, Robert Estienne, who made the verse divisions, is said to have made some of these while riding horseback. Looking at some of the divisions we might well ask whether he sometimes divided sentences according to the jog of his horse! We need to discover a sense of the whole Bible's story.

5. *We have trouble with the language.* The seventeenth century English of the King James era just doesn't sound like the English we speak today.

> Example: 1 Corinthians 13:4, 5 KJV, "Charity suffereth long, and is kind; charity envieth not; charity vaunteth not itself, is not puffed up, doth not behave itself unseemly. . . ."

The English language is a living language and is constantly changing. New translations of the Bible are made to put the message of the Bible into the language we speak and understand. The New English Bible (1961) translates 1 Corinthians 13:4, 5:

"Love is patient; love is kind and envies no one. Love is never boastful, nor conceited, nor rude; never selfish, not quick to take offence."

6. *Maybe we haven't found Bible study exciting.* We may remember when we *had* to memorize verses, or *had* to go to Sunday school to hear the same old stories, or the long Scripture readings by the minister.

Does this describe some of your experiences with the Bible? Maybe you've gotten past some of these problems and have found that the Bible speaks to you. Good for you if you have. But if the Bible doesn't mean much to you, where can you begin?

WHAT IS THE BIBLE?

The Bible came to us in a two-volume form called the Old and the New Testament. Testament, or the other term often used in this two-part title, covenant, reminds us that this book has to do with a binding relationship. Here is the story of man's perennial problem of sticking by a binding relationship. But here too is man's recognition that he is secure only in such a relationship with God.

The Old Testament comes out of the religious experience of persons living before Abraham, and then the Hebrew people whose story begins nearly 1900 years before Jesus. The New Testament is the story of Jesus, and the beginning of the Christian church during the first century of the Christian era.

Most of the Old Testament writings had been written and gathered by 200 B.C. But it was a council of Jewish rabbis, meeting at Jamnia, Palestine, about A.D. 90 that decided no more books should be admitted to the group of sacred writings. This group of thirty-nine books was included according to the following division:

(1)	(2)	(3)
The Law	*The Prophets*	*The Writings*
Genesis	Former Prophets: Joshua,	Psalms, Job,
Exodus	Judges, 1 and 2 Samuel,	Proverbs, Ruth,
Leviticus	1 and 2 Kings	Song of Solomon

Numbers	Latter Prophets: Isaiah,	Ecclesiastes
Deuteronomy	Jeremiah, Ezekiel, the	Lamentations
	Twelve Minor Prophets	Esther
	(Hosea, Joel, Amos, Oba-	Daniel
	diah, Jonah, Micah, Nahum,	Ezra, Nehemiah
	Habakkuk, Zephaniah, Hag-	1 & 2 Chronicles
	gai, Zechariah, Malachi)	

Check the table of contents of your Bible to see how the Hebrew Bible differs from our Old Testament.

The Old Testament was the sacred book used by Jesus and the early Christians. Later there were added the letters of Paul to the churches; letters of other Christian leaders; the Gospels, which retold the story of Jesus; and a history of the early church, the Acts of the Apostles.

Other writings, like the Letter to the Hebrews and Revelation were written during the persecution of the Christians, and testify to the bravery of the early Christians as they stood firm against a hostile world.

Still other writings began to be circulated toward the end of the first century and during the second century. Because not all of these were on a par with the books now in our New Testament, a list of accepted writings called "the canon" came into being. *Canon* is a Greek word meaning rule or standard of measurement. These books, through their use in the church, became the rule or standard of Christian faith and life. Actually this complete list of twenty-seven appeared first in a letter by Bishop Athanasius to members of his parish in A.D. 367.

WHY THE MESSAGE OF THE BIBLE IS SO IMPORTANT

The body of writings we know as the Bible came to be regarded as uniquely inspired by God in a way that no other writings before or since are inspired, because of its witness to Jesus Christ.

The story of the Hebrew people is a recounting of God's redemptive acts in history. It is also an interpretation of what these events mean. Jesus came at the end of a long period of preparation. The New Testament tells how God showed himself most clearly in the person of Jesus (Jn. 3:16 and Heb. 1:1, 2), and how the church is the continuation of Christ's work upon the earth (Eph. 1:15-23).

But there is more. The Bible makes it clear that God made himself known not merely to give us some bits of information. To the writers of the Bible, knowing God is not merely discovering facts about Him. The word *know* means more than gaining a certain amount of factual information. The word *know* also means "to experience." More than knowing a name, or face, or a few facts about someone, we *know* when we have entered into relationship, and experience the friendship of someone.

This is the purpose set forth by the writer of the Fourth Gospel: *These are written* (and we would today add, "These are translated, taught, and preached") *that you may believe that Jesus is the Christ, the Son of God, and that believing, you may have life in his name* (Jn. 20:31).

The Bible Speaks to You

In one of Von Schlegel's plays, the curtain rises to show the inside of a theater where another audience is waiting for the curtain to rise. When it does, there is a second such scene; then

Is the audience on stage?

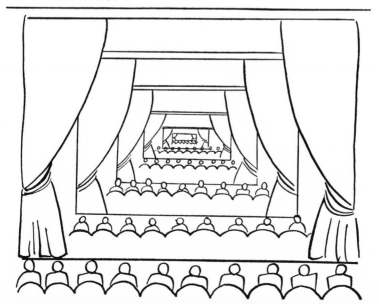

a third. By this time the original audience begins to grow uneasy and looks around to see if perhaps it too is on the stage. This should happen when we open the pages of the Bible.

It is *we* who are tempted to be like God,
> not just Adam and Eve (Gen. 3:1-6).

It is *we* who are in danger of religion that becomes only form,
> not just the scribes and the Pharisees (Mt. 23).

It is *we* to whom the invitation of the kingdom comes . . .
> not just to the people living in the Palestinian villages
> around the year A.D. 30 (Mk. 1:15).

It is *we* who are called to be *children of God* . . .
> *working together with him,*
> not just Peter and Paul and Timothy and a few others living
> way back there (Jn. 1:12; 2 Cor. 6:1).

From beginning to end, there is a Word here which refuses to be dismissed as something God said once long ago. Here is a Word that insists on being heard as what God is saying now, and to you. You open this book at your peril. But to keep it closed is to deny yourself the adventure of life with God!

WHEN YOU STUDY THE BIBLE

1. Read the Bible conscious of its central theme of covenant written right into the title of its two parts. God through His Son Jesus Christ has entered a binding covenant to love sinning man to the very end. Martin Luther said, "When reading the Bible, take Christ with you, for He is the one whom everything concerns."

2. Recognize the Bible as a collection of books. Try to discover the characteristics of the different books and how they relate to the main theme.

3. Use "the five P's" of Bible study. In dealing with a particular section, try to find out, insofar as possible, (a) the person by whom written, (b) the person to whom written, (c) the place from which written, (d) the period at which written, (e) the purpose for which written (J. Carter Swaim).

4. Study the Bible with others. Many eyes and minds together see more than only one sees.

5. Use other aids:

A *Bible dictionary* can help you with the meanings of worc like faith, grace, and reconciliation. Here, too, you can find information on names, places, and customs.

A *concordance,* which lists the words used in the Bible, will help you find where and how these words are used.

A *commentary* has an introduction to each book of the Bible, and will help with the more difficult passages.

Do not hesitate to ask your pastor about these and other aids for your Bible study.

6. Read the Bible in different translations. The Revised Standard Version of 1952 has found wide use, as has the New English Bible (New Testament, 1961). In addition there are other translations and paraphrases, like the American Bible Society's *Good News for Modern Man* (1966) and J. B. Phillips' *The New Testament in Modern English* (1958). The task of translating God's word into man's language will continue as long as word use changes and men consider the Bible permanently trustworthy as the story of God's love. Read these new translations for clarity and freshness.

Chapter 4

What Is God Like?

. . . one God and Father of us all, who is above all and through all and in all.   Ephesians 4:6

A little girl was busily engaged with a pencil and a piece of paper. Her mother looked over her shoulder and asked, "What are you drawing?" "I'm drawing a picture of God," was the reply. "But," the mother said, "nobody knows what God looks like." "They will, when I get through," said the little girl.

In the preceding pages we referred to a God who is making himself known to people—through nature, conscience, the experiences of men now as well as in the past, the church, and the Bible. In session one we noted this God has a purpose and plan for persons (Eph. 1:10-12). What else do we believe about God?

TEST YOURSELF

What do you think Christians believe about God?

T   F   God demands that we fear Him.
T   F   God's chief job is to bail us out when we are in trouble.
T   F   God has absolute power over mankind.
T   F   God is known through wisdom.
T   F   God created this world.

There is no one simple definition of what God is like. From our own experience and from what others have said, we have ideas of what God is like. Who is God? What is He like?

DISCOVERIES ABOUT GOD

Our understanding of God comes from the experiences men have had with God. Here are several landmarks in man's understanding of what God has revealed about himself:

1. *God is.* From earliest times men have felt a sense of mystery in the world surrounding them. The mysteries primitive man found most baffling were death, unusual events in nature, sickness, and wild animals. In each of these things which they could not explain, they saw a supernatural spirit, a god at work. They believed there were good spirits and evil spirits.

This sense of "something beyond themselves" led them to develop a system of religion which included:

The setting aside of certain objects as sacred because these could provide blessings.

The worship of spirits in nature (storms, plants, trees, the moon).

Worship of ancestor spirits.

The practice of magic and sacrifice to control or at least pacify these forces.

Development of a mythology which provided reasons for beliefs.[4]

Consider the way in which religion developed in ancient Babylonia. As the people changed from hunters and fishers to city dwellers, their beliefs in gods of the fields and streams changed to a highly organized system of gods. The Babylonians believed in gods who were very much like themselves but with supernatural powers. This religion finally included belief in "Marduk," lord of the gods, to whom they built a shrine in Babylon.

2. *God is one God.* As the Babylonians came to think of Marduk as God of the gods, so also among other religions men came to think of a chief god. The Hindus of ancient India believed in a great many gods. But over all these gods they set Brahma, the supreme God. For Hindus, Brahma constitutes the entire universe. They believe Brahma came into existence before anything else and is still the essence of everything.

But it was through the Hebrew people that the recognition that God is one God came most clearly. The story of the Hebrew people begins nearly four thousand years ago with Abraham. You can read it beginning at Genesis 12.

Abraham appeared first in the region of the river valleys of central Asia. There in those countries beneath the wide sky men watched and worshiped the moon. But Abraham was not satisfied.

At the call of God, Abraham came from the East with his wife, Sarah, and nephew, Lot. Over the plains and past the hills they came, entering the little strip of country lying between the Mediterranean Sea and the Jordan River. Canaan, the land was then called. Wherever they pitched their tents, Abraham built altars of stone and worshiped God.

From that journey of faith came the conviction that God would bless Abraham, and use him to bless all peoples.

In the years that followed, persons grew in their understanding of God. Abraham's descendants, Isaac, Jacob, and Joseph, and the tribe of people that came to be known as the children of Israel, saw God acting in their experiences.

When Moses led the Hebrews out of Egypt after four hundred years, they saw it as God's act of deliverance. What other conclusion could they have reached when the personal experience of Moses' call to deliver, God's wind at work on the waters, and the miraculous escape of the oppressed slaves all pointed to God? Their song of God's triumph is preserved for us in Exodus 15. Note especially verses 11-13.

For forty more years the Hebrews moved about and lived in the wilderness of the Sinai Penninsula before their return into Canaan. During this time they received commandments about their relationship to God. The first of these was: *"I am the Lord your God, who brought you out of the land of Egypt, out of the house of bondage. You shall have no other gods before me"* (Ex. 20:2, 3).

This understanding of God was reinforced by later experiences, and the first lesson that Hebrews taught their children was: *Hear, O Israel: The Lord our God is one Lord; and you shall love the Lord your God . . .* (Deut. 6:4, 5).

3. *God is the God of history.* The Hebrews believed that God was with them in their escape from Egypt, in their entry into Canaan, and in their becoming a nation. Under King David (1000 B.C.) and his son, Solomon, they became a powerful and

wealthy nation. But then, as a series of tragedies shook the Hebrew nation, the people began to wonder, "Has God forgotten us?"

The historical books of Samuel and the Kings, and later, the Chronicles, were written to help people understand that God was also God of the judgments of history. Here is one example: *When the rule of Rehoboam was established and was strong, he forsook the law of the Lord, and all Israel with him . . . because they had been unfaithful to the Lord, Shishak king of Egypt came up against Jerusalem . . . (2 Chron. 12:1, 2).*

As the people of Israel were going through these experiences, the prophets were trying to interpret God to the people. The prophets said that God acted as He did in the affairs of His people because of who and what He is. Claims of the prophets included these ideas:

GOD IS HOLY, RIGHTEOUS AND JUST

That is, He is separate from men, mysterious, and powerful.

For I am God and not man, the Holy One in your midst (Hos. 11:9). God is righteous.

He will judge the world with righteousness, and the peoples with equity (Ps. 98:9).

Or read here the prophecies of Amos about God's justice.

GOD IS IN CONTROL.

Have you not known? . . . It is he who sits above the circle of the earth . . . and makes the rulers of the earth as nothing (Is. 40:21-23).

GOD IS GOD OVER ALL MEN, ALL NATIONS.

After the Hebrew nation had been broken up, and many of the people scattered to different countries, the prophets helped them understand that God was not only a "Hebrew God," but God of all (Is. 45:1).

4. *God is the God of mercy and love.* Hosea was one of Israel's prophets who lived about 750 B.C. To illustrate God's ways with men Hosea described a painful personal experience. Hosea's

wife, Gomer, had left him. But he could not forget her. Finally, he found her at the auction where they sold slaves. He bid, and bought her back, and took her home again to live with him.

So, Hosea said, God will yet be merciful to His faithless people. So God's love works in and through His righteousness seeking to bring men to repentance, seeking to redeem men from their sin.

I will heal their faithlessness;
I will love them freely,
for my anger has turned from them (Hos. 14:4).

The New Testament gives us this picture of God too. It is through the person of Jesus that we see God most clearly, as the God of mercy and love. Jesus reveals God's justice too. But the good news made so plain in Jesus is that God is more than a holy judge. God is also love and mercy!

For God so loved the world that he gave his only Son,
that whoever believes in him should not perish but have
eternal life (Jn. 3:16).

The word *Father* was often on Jesus' lips when He talked about God. The great parable of God's love for us is that story Jesus told about the prodigal son and the forgiving Father (Lk. 15: 11-24).

For the first Christians, it was the amazing love of God that brought power into their lives and changed their attitudes toward all men (1 Jn. 4:7-12).

A DESCRIPTION OF GOD: THE TRINITY

Paul ends a letter to the Corinthians with the words, *The grace of the Lord Jesus Christ and the love of God and the fellowship of the Holy Spirit be with you all* (2 Cor. 13:14). What did he mean? Are God, Christ, the Holy Spirit, all the same, or are they different? And what did the church later mean by the formula known as the Trinity?

About A.D. 200 the idea of the Trinity began to be used by the church as a description of God. The idea is that God shows himself in three persons or forms: Father, Son, and Holy Spirit. Tertullian, a Christian of A.D. 200, thought of it as being like

The disciples discovered continuing power through the Holy Spirit.

27

three different officials carrying out three different tasks in one and the same government. Athanasius, a hundred years later, likened it to the fact that the same man can be at the same time a father, a son, and a brother.

But behind the Trinity, and these attempts to illustrate it, lay the experience of the early Christians. So rich and full was their experience of God that no single statement could describe it.

Think of Peter and his encounter with God. As a Hebrew by birth and training, he learned about the God of the Hebrews, a God who is holy and just, and who demands obedience. Then one day Peter met Jesus, and was called to leave his fishnet, and become a disciple. Peter learned what God's love is like as he lived and worked with Jesus. After the resurrection and ascension of Jesus, Peter discovered the living continuing power of God in his life through the Holy Spirit (Acts 2) even though Jesus was no longer present in the form of a physical person.

In Old Testament times already the people believed God was near His people. They believed His presence was over the ark of the covenant, or that God was in the cloud over the tabernacle. In Jesus, God came in the form of a person. *Emmanuel,* that name given Jesus, means "God with us" (Mt. 1:23). Then after Jesus' ascension, it became unmistakably clear that God continued to live with men in a most intimate way. That God is *near* us, and *with* us, and even now *in* us by His Spirit is the ringing faith of the New Testament and the church.

THINK ABOUT THIS

1. Can man *discover* what God is like, or can we speak of understanding God only as God reveals himself to man?

2. How do we account for a kind of progression in man's understanding of who God is?

3. Are we in danger of assuming that we know too much or too little about God? Note the comment by W. F. Albright, noted archaeologist and authority on the Old Testament, in referring to the Bible as God's culminating revelation to man.

"At least a hundred thousand years had elapsed since man first learned to make artifacts—less than two thousand years have passed since the close of the canon. Yet some ask us to believe that the Bible reflects so primitive a stage . . . that it no longer has meaning for modern man!"[5]

David Cairns tells of coming back from a fishing trip with his father and mother. He had a fishing line which had gotten into a desperate tangle. Finally, his father, who had been watching him, said, "Let me try it, David."

He handed it over, and like magic the line spread out in his father's hands, and he got it back about as good as ever in two or three minutes.

The son's comment made years later was: "Neither of us had any idea that we were giving or getting a picture that would be with me at least all my days to show how God deals with His children and how we should deal with Him."[6]

A PRAYER

For all that we know of Thee in Christ, O God, we give Thee thanks; and for all that Thou art in Him, which is beyond our knowing. Amen.[7]

4. Robert B. Laurin, *When God Judges* (Valley Forge: Judson Press, 1964), pp. 118, 119.

5. W. F. Albright, "Recent Discoveries in Bible Lands," *Supplement to Young's Analytical Concordance to the Bible* (22nd ed., Grand Rapids: Wm. B. Eerdmans, 1955), p. 51.

6. Robert J. McCracken, *Questions People Ask* (New York: Harper and Brothers, 1951), p. 26.

7. Paul Scherer, *The Word God Sent* (New York: Harper and Row, 1965), p. 153.

Chapter 5

God -- the Creator

*By faith we understand that the world was created by the word
of God. . . .*   Hebrews 11:3

"In my travels around the earth I saw no God or angels,"
Soviet cosmonaut Titov reported. American astronaut John
Glenn's reply was: "The God I pray to is not so small that I
expected to see Him in space."

How big is God? How much room is there in your understanding of God for the facts about the world in which we live? What
about the claims of the astronomers that the farthest stars that can
be observed by our telescopes are over one hundred million light
years distant from the earth? Or that our little solar system (the
sun, earth, moon, and observable planets) is but one of many,

How big is God?

perhaps millions of solar systems that extend farther than our most powerful telescope can see?

Is there room in your understanding of God for the evidence cited by geologists that rocks a million, or ten million years old, containing fossils of prehistoric plants and animals, point to a much older age of the earth than we used to think? What do we make of the claims of biologists that plants and animals, over a period of generations and centuries, change and develop . . .?

To the Hebrews, to whom God revealed himself as one God, it became clear that this God was acting in their life as a people. But a further important belief about God became apparent. The one God, the ruler of all things, is also *the Creator of all things*. Isaiah 45:18 is an example of this belief about God:

> *For thus says the Lord,*
> *who created the heavens*
> *   (he is God!),*
> *who formed the earth and made it*
> *   (he established it;*
> *he did not create it a chaos,*
> *   he formed it to be inhabited!):*
> *I am the Lord, and there is no other.*

God is the Creator! This is the message declared in Genesis chapters 1 and 2, to which we now turn.

HOW DO YOU READ GENESIS 1?

1. Read Genesis 1:1—2:3 underlining the name *God* every time it appears. How many times is it used? What does this say to you about the writer's purpose?

2. List the steps in creation as recorded in Genesis 1.

verses 1-10	verses 20-23
verses 11-13	verses 24, 25
verses 14-19	verses 26-28

Notice the progression. How does this correspond with or differ from scientific descriptions of the development of the earth?

3. What does the writer describe as the climax of creation (vv. 26-28)?

What distinguishes man from the rest of the creation (v. 27)?

How do you understand the tasks given to man as outlined in verse 28?

4. What does Genesis 1:31 say about God's creation?

5. Now read Genesis 2:4-25. Note that here is a second telling of the creation, especially the creation of man. At this point, how would you write in a sentence or two the theme of Genesis 1 and 2? What do you think is the writer's purpose in this story?

NOTES ON READING GENESIS

A difficulty for modern readers of the creation stories arose about one hundred years ago when scientists began to point out that the world had taken millions, perhaps billions of years to develop into its present form. But the Bible spoke of creation in six "days." Besides this, many of the copies of the Bible had the date 4004 B.C. in the margin as the date of creation. Who was right, science or the Bible?

To ask the question this way (as we usually do) is to miss the point. The question we must really ask is: What is the purpose of these creation stories? The writer, living in a prescientific day, looks at the world in which he lives. His answer to the question of "Why the World?" is "God." God created it! God in His greatness and love brought the world into being. These are stories praising God. Here is a message to people who were constantly tempted to resort to the paganism of nature worship. Here is the reminder that the God of being, the God who revealed himself to Abraham and Isaac and Jacob and Moses is the God of all creation!

It is at the point of the author's description of how God did all this, that science raises the questions. For science investigates answers to the question, How? These creation stories were based on the scientific information available in those centuries B.C. For example, the Bible writers took for granted a three-level view of the universe: heaven, earth, and underworld. According to this view the earth is a flat surface. Above the earth, like a huge dome, is the firmament in which are hung the sun and moon and stars.

The earth is founded upon pillars which are sunk into subterranean waters. This underworld is a mysterious place, the dwelling of the dead.

Copernicus and Galileo asserted that the earth is not the center of the universe but a little satellite that goes around the sun. Constantly we are learning more about the universe in which we live. Perhaps the people of another generation will look back at our time and say, "How prescientific they were back there in the twentieth century!"

The fact that our scientific knowledge about the world in which we live has changed considerably since Genesis was written does not undercut or disprove the *religious* insights of the authors.

God created is the affirmation of these creation stories. Science cannot prove or disprove that religious truth. Yet great scientists have affirmed it.

On the question of creation in six 24-hour days, remember that the Bible also says "one day is with the Lord as a thousand years." And that 4004 B.C. date never was a part of the early manuscripts of the Bible. That date got into the Bible's margin as the theory of Archbishop James Ussher, about A.D. 1650. He arrived at the date of creation by counting back the generations mentioned in Genesis chapters 5 and 11. This method is no longer accepted as an accurate method to determine the age of the earth.

CHANCE OR CREATION?

But for many the question still persists. If we look upon the Bible's stories of creation as religious truth, and accept modern science's descriptions of the development of the world, does this not destroy or weaken the belief that God created?

A. Cressy Morrison, former president of the New York Academy of Science, speaks of this in his book, *Man Does Not Stand Alone* (New York: Fleming H. Revell Co., 1944). If our earth rotated at one tenth of its present rate, our days and nights would be increased tenfold. As a result during the long days the sun would burn up all the vegetation. During the nights the temperatures would drop to a point so low that it would freeze any plant life that survived the day.

Dr. Morrison reminds us that we are at just the right distance from the sun. If the sun were farther away, the earth would be too cold to sustain life. If we were a bit closer to the sun, we would all roast in a solar furnace.

Today we are concerned with landing men on a moon that is 240,000 miles away. Morrison points out that if our moon were "only 50,000 miles away . . . our tides would be so enormous that twice a day all continents would be submerged."

If the crust of our earth were merely ten feet thicker, the metallic elements in the crust would combine with all the free oxygen in the atmosphere. This would completely rule out the possibility of animal life on the planet.

Likewise if the ocean were merely a few feet deeper, it would absorb so much carbon dioxide from the air that plants could not exist.

Morrison concludes: "There is not one chance in millions that life on our planet is by accident."

The French scientist, Lecomte duNouy, examined the mathematical odds of life having evolved by chance from nonliving material. He calculated the possibility of the formation of a single protein molecule by chance. DuNouy concluded that the odds against the formation of a single protein molecule were so large as to be virtually impossible. He reported that "the time needed to form, on an average, one such molecule in a material volume equal to that of our terrestrial globe is about 10^{243} billions of years."[8] (This is equivalent to one billion followed by 243 zeros.)

These are the "chances" for *one protein molecule* to develop. A single cell needs millions of these and other complex molecules. And a single human body is made up of millions of cells.

The Christian faith says, "not chance, but God." The world came into being not by chance. But the same God who makes himself known to people, also made the world and the persons who inhabit the earth.

WHAT THE CREATION STORIES ARE ALL ABOUT

Belief in God as the Creator affirms these truths:

1. God is the ruler. To say that God made the earth is to confess that it belongs to Him. He is its Lord.

The earth is the Lord's and the fulness thereof,
the world and those who dwell therein;
for he has founded it . . ." (Ps. 24:1, 2).

2. All that is, is dependent upon God. I too am a creation of God. I am not the master of my life. God is. We have not placed ourselves here. God has. *It is he that made us, and we are his* (Ps. 100:3).

3. God's world is good. God did not create the earth as a chaos. He formed it to be man's dwelling place. He made it so that it might be beautiful, useful, and good (Gen. 1:3). We are not trapped in an unfriendly and hostile universe. We do not need to try to escape it, but we can enjoy God's world.

4. There is meaning and purpose in God's creation. The world in which we live didn't "just happen." God has a plan for it, and a purpose for us in it (Eph. 1:9, 10).

5. God has given man a special place in His creation. Man is made to have fellowship with God. He is the only creature who can answer God, either in defiance or in trust. Our lives are made for conversation with God, and for work together with Him. This is true for every person . . . *the people whom I formed for myself that they might declare my praise* (Is. 43:21).

6. All men are one in creation. *He made from one every nation of men to live on all the face of the earth . . .* (Acts 17:26). The arguments that God made some races superior to other races are not Christian arguments.

7. We understand the meaning and purpose of creation best through Jesus Christ. *All things were created through him and for him* (Col. 1:16). The Christian belief is that through Jesus Christ God continues to work creatively in this world. Colossians 1:17-20 speaks of this.

HOW WILL YOU RESPOND TO GOD'S CREATION?

1. Clip and bring to class several newspaper articles or stories that point to the misuse of God's creation. Also look for stories that point to man's cooperation with God in creation.

2. In what ways is war a denial of God's creation?

3. In the 1930's Adolf Hitler expounded the theory of a superior race as justification for the systematic slaughter of six million Jews. Several years later, on the west coast of the United States and Canada, thousands of Japanese people, and American and Canadian citizens of Japanese background, found their property confiscated as they were herded together into detention camps. Even more recently the Negro and the Indian have often been excluded from the human race by their white neighbors. In what way does the doctrine of creation speak to these problems of prejudice?

4. Which do you think is most important? Why?
    To know the exact year when the earth was formed
    To learn to live together on God's earth
    To land a man on the moon

5. Is there room in your thinking for the possibilities that God is still creating, and that He is using man in His creative acts? How might God be planning to use you?

PRAYER

O Thou who hast ordered this wondrous world and who knowest all things on earth and heaven: So fill our hearts with trust in Thee that by night and by day, at all times and in all seasons, we may without fear commit ourselves and those who are dear to us to Thy never-failing love, for this life and the life to come. Amen.[9]

8. Pierre Lecomte du Nouy. *Human Destiny* (New York: New American Library, 1947), p. 34.

9. *The Book of Common Worship* (Board of Christian Education of the Presbyterian Church in the United States of America, 1946).

Chapter 6

God's Care for His World

O Lord, how manifold are thy works!
In wisdom hast thou made them all;
the earth is full of thy creatures . . .
These all look to thee,
to give them their food in due season.
When thou givest to them, they gather it up;
when thou openest thy hand, they are filled
with good things.
When thou hidest thy face, they are dismayed;
when thou takest away their breath, they die
and return to their dust.
When thou sendest forth thy Spirit,
they are created;
and thou renewest the face of the ground.

Psalm 104:24, 27-30

VIEWS OF GOD'S RELATION TO THE WORLD

Many people share the belief that God created the world. But not all agree on the "how" of God's creation. An old Hindu belief has it that the world came into being as a result of the jealous warring of the gods. Others have said that once the world and its laws were established, the God who created it withdrew from the scene and simply let the world carry on by itself, a view called *deism*. Still others have said that the world *is* God, that there is no difference between the Maker and the processes that He set in motion, a view called *pantheism*.

Over against these ideas is the Christian belief that God has not withdrawn himself from His world. God is also *Emmanuel,*

"God with us" (Is. 7:14; Mt. 1:23). God is in this world with His concern, even now. He who made the world continues to work in it and through it, and has purpose for man, whom He has placed in the world. Could it be that the real purpose of the Bible's creation story is to indicate what God is doing all the time?

HOW DOES GOD CARE FOR HIS WORLD?
All Creation Looks to God! (Ps. 104).

The writer of Psalm 104 did not live in a city of steel and concrete. He knew the feel of wind in his face, and the gentle warmth of the springtime sun. He knew what it was to lie on soft, green grass, to watch the soaring birds, and to observe the gentle movement of clouds overhead. He thrilled to the sound of the mountain brook racing on its way to the valleys. He enjoyed the jumping of the mountain goats, grazing and climbing the steep slopes. The earth he saw around him, so vibrant with life, spoke to him of God's care. All that he saw was a call to praise God!

A READING PROJECT

1. God, the purposeful Creator:

Read through verses 1-9, listing what the psalmist sees in the world around him that speaks to him of God's greatness.

2. God's orderly care for His creation:

As you read verses 10-30, make a list of the evidences given for God's continuing care for the world.

Example: v. 10—the springs of water to feed the wildlife

v. 13—the rain

v. 14—

What other evidences of God's continuing care for the world can you think of that are not listed here?

3. The psalmist's conclusion and praise:

In a sentence, describe the psalmist's reaction to what he sees of God in the world in which he lives (vv. 31-35).

What do you make of verse 35? Is wicked man the one sour note in the symphony of creation?

THE BALANCE OF NATURE

Sometimes the impression is given that only God's acts are "supernatural." When we can explain the sun's rising in the east because of the rotation of the earth, or an eclipse of the sun because of the moon's getting in our line of vision, we say, "These are the laws of nature." But God acts in a unity of spirit and nature. God does not ordinarily bypass the laws of nature.

Is it by accident, by natural instinct, or by a Creator-infused instinct that the creatures live? Consider the wasp. A wasp will overpower a grasshopper, dig a hole in the earth, and sting the grasshopper in exactly the right place so that he does not die but becomes unconscious and lives on, a form of preserved meat. Then the wasp will lay its eggs so that its children when they hatch can nibble without killing the insect on which they feed. For them dead meat would be fatal. The mother then dies; she never sees her young.[10]

Others have seen God's care in the fact that there are "checks" in the world of nature. The common thrush is an example. The thrush begins to produce eggs when it is one year old, and its average length of life is about ten years. Every year a pair of thrushes will rear two broods, each consisting of about four nestlings. If the offspring of a single pair all survived and mated, at the end of the tenth year, there would be a population of $19\frac{1}{2}$ million. In another ten years these would grow to nearly 200 million million. Soon there would not be room enough for all the thrushes on the entire surface of the earth.[11]

What is it that keeps herring from speedily choking up all the seas of the world? Or why do flies not grow to the size of elephants, or ants become the size of lions?

MAN—CARETAKER OF GOD'S WORLD

Not only does God work through the laws of nature. God also uses man as a partner in taking care of the created world. This is the meaning of the words about having *dominion . . . over every living thing that moves upon the earth* (Gen. 1:28).

This is the meaning of man being put *in the garden of Eden to till it and keep it* (Gen. 2:15).

Creation points up the fact that God is the ultimate owner of the earth (Ps. 24:1). The Bible makes it clear that we are stewards, caretakers, managers of His estate. Jesus told several parables about stewards to point out how we are responsible to God for the gifts of time and talent and possessions given us (Mt. 18:23-35; Lk. 16:1-16; 12:42-48).

How does God use us in caring for His world? In our world, God has many good and exciting things He wants done. He fills the earth with oil and coal and metals, but it takes brains to get them out and make use of them. God fills the earth with secret powers that, in season, give us wheat, corn, fruits, and nuts; but we have to do our part.

George Washington Carver, one of the great Christian men of our time, made this discovery. He grew up among the poor farmers of the South. He became convinced that the farmers needed to diversify their crops by planting soil-enriching peanuts instead of soil-exhausting cotton. He prayed to God: "Lord, show me what I can do with a peanut." He said God answered that earnest little prayer of his by saying: "You have brains; find out!"

So George Washington Carver set to work. Using the brains that God had put into his head, he devoted his life to agricultural research. From the peanut he learned how to make cheese, milk, coffee, flour, ink, dyes, soap, wood stains, and nearly three hundred other products.

Were George Washington Carver's discoveries of the uses of the peanut an accident? Was the improved life of the poor farmers of the South due to these discoveries, coincidence? Or was God working through George Washington Carver?

Can a farmer, bus driver, check-out clerk, carhop, bank teller, nurse, welder, or teacher feel that God is using him or her as a "caretaker" of His world? What does it take to make a vocation God-cooperating? Can you think of vocations that God cannot use?

A major problem facing our world is hunger and a rapidly

increasing population. By 1830 there were 1 billion people on earth. By 1930 there were 2 billion. By 1960 there were 3 billion. By the year 2000, there may be as many as 6 billion.

Is it possible to believe that God is working through the technology of our time? Think of the miracles of food production brought about by fertilizer, irrigation, new machines, and new methods of processing and preserving food so it may be distributed to areas of need.

Some food experts visualize fish herded and raised in offshore pens as cattle are today. Huge fields of kelp and other kinds of seaweed will be tended by undersea farmers. The protein-rich underseas crop will provide a nourishing cereal in a variety of flavors through chemical treatment.[12]

Currently there are men working on producing protein in the science laboratories. If protein can be developed so the process of making it is inexpensive, about two-thirds of the world might be able to have a manufactured protein steak for supper instead of being hungry and undernourished.

God does not necessarily bypass man and his brain and the science labs in caring for His world!

LET THE WICKED BE NO MORE!

Psalm 104:35 reminds us, however, that we are not automatically God's workers. Because of selfishness man often becomes careless destroyer.

Marya Mannes writes of this: "Cans. Beer cans. Glinting on the verges of a million miles of roadways, lying in scrub, grass, dirt, leaves, sand, mud, but never hidden. Piels, Rheingold, Ballantine, Schaefer, Schlitz, shining in the sun or picked by moon or the beams of headlights at night: washed by rain or flattened by wheels, but never dulled, never buried, never destroyed. Here is the mark of savages, the testament of wasters, the stain of prosperity."

"What kind of people are these," Miss Mannes asks, "people who drink—and discard a million tons of metal, who demand that forests be cut down to wrap and seal what they eat and smoke

Wasters impoverish our land.

and chew, who need thirty feet of steel and two hundred horse-power to take them to their small destinations? Destroying beauty with their hideous signs, they leave the carcasses of cars to rot in heaps, spill their trash into ravines, and choke off the life in the rivers and lakes with the waste of their produce."

"Who is as rich as that?" she asks. "Slowly the wasters and despoilers are impoverishing our land, our nature, our beauty, so that there will not be one beach, one hill, one lane, one meadow, one forest free from the debris of man and the stigma of his improvidence. Who is so rich that he can squander forever the wealth of earth and water for the trivial needs of vanity or the compulsive demands of greed . . . ?"[13]

To this kind of waste-making of God's world, we can add war and others.

The generating of fears that set men to explode the bombs that fill the atmosphere with deadly strontium 90, with no regard for the future generations.

The costly race to the planets and moon primarily for military advantage and prestige.

The expending of $120 billion by the nations of the world for weapons and soldiers, while people starve for lack of food.

The slaughter of the best of the youth in war.

The making of homeless refugees by thousands and hundreds of thousands.

The waste in natural resources, and the effects of brutalizing people . . . of making a virtue out of killing and destroying.

What other kinds of waste-making do you think of?

IS MAN ALONE GOD'S MESSENGER?

Does God depend only on man to care for His world? The Hebrews also believed that there were supernatural beings as God's helpers (Gen. 28:12). The word *angel* comes from Hebrew and Greek words that mean "messenger." In the early Old Testament books the most common use is "the angel of the Lord" (Gen. 16:7). The idea is that of a being who brought a message from God, or the phrase is used to describe how God spoke to people.

The largest number of references to angels is found in the writings between the Old and New Testaments. At a time when God seemed far away, it was necessary to weave elaborate theories about how He retained control of His universe.

Angels are spoken of in the Gospels, in Acts, and in the New Testament letters. Here they are often bringers of special news from God (Lk. 1:11-20; 2:8-14). The Pharisees and Sadducees of Jesus' day were not in agreement about belief in angels (Acts 23:6-8).

The Orthodox churches believe that each individual has a guardian angel. A Greek Orthodox Church litany includes: "For an angel of peace, a faithful guide, a guardian of our souls and bodies, let us beseech the Lord." Sabine Baring-Gould's evening hymn, based on Proverbs 3:24, contains the lines:

> "Through the long night watches,
> May thine angels spread
> Their white wings above me,
> Watching round my bed."

There is no reason to think that angels do not exist. Since Christ came, however, there seems to be less need for the ministry of angels. We do not need angels to carry our prayers to God. In Jesus Christ we become children of the Father. And God's presence is made known to us in the Holy Spirit. Emmanuel! God is with us! If God is with us, we can then also believe that God uses us as messengers of His provident care.

WORDS TO REMEMBER

Theism. The Christian understanding of God as the Creator who made the world, but also the One who controls its processes.

Providence. Divine guidance or care.

Angel. A good spirit; messenger of God.

GOD'S CARE FOR HIS WORLD TODAY

1. What would you say is most meaningful to you of any of the evidences that God is concerned about us and cares for us?

2. Do you think God has a place for the city in His providing for the world? Why or why not? Do you think of ways in which the modern city is being used of God for His purposes?

3. Does God have a unique role for persons living in rural areas in caring for the world?

4. Do you think that God is in the revolutions of our day? What do you see as His concern for or relation to poverty and hunger? Toward racial clashes? Toward the rise and spread of communism?

A PRAYER

O God, I thank You for placing me into such a world. Help me to trust in Your care for this world, and to become a faithful worker with You in caring for all You have given. Amen.

10. A. Cressy Morrison, *Reader's Digest,* 49:296 (December 1946), p. 13.
11. J. W. N. Sullivan, *The Limitation of Science* (New York: The New American Library, 1949), p. 85.
12. *Time* (February 25, 1966), p. 28.
13. Marya Mannes, *More in Anger* (Philadelphia: J. B. Lippincott Company, 1958), pp. 40, 41.

Chapter 7

The Problem of Evil

And God saw everything that he had made, and behold, it was
   very good. Genesis 1:31
God is love. 1 John 4:8

WHAT ABOUT THIS?

Anxious ears listen as the radio crackles with static, "The Kansas City weather bureau has issued a severe weather warning for an area 60 miles on either side of a line starting from Dodge City . . . possibility of strong winds, hail, and several tornadoes from the present time until 9 P.M. . . ."

Uneasy eyes scan the clouds to the west. People hurry about. Now a sheet of gray is visible less than a mile away. At 6:14 the storm comes screaming in. Wind, rain, hail, sweeps across the area. Within an hour the storm's fury has moved on, and the settling sun's rays break through beneath the clouds. Now a rainbow is clearly visible. But so too are the broken trees, the downed power lines, the scattered boards and bricks of houses . . . a battered car . . . a refrigerator deposited in a backyard . . . shredded bedding and clothing . . . Toll: 3 dead, 21 injured, $1 million or more in property damage.

Or, what about this?

"Dad, do you think I can go into Pax as Jim did?" asked fourteen-year-old Bill. The Martens family had hurried home after church. Mother headed for the kitchen. Bill could tell that Mother and Dad were proud of Jim tonight as he spoke to the church. "I want to thank my parents and all of you in the church who made it possible for me to spend these two years in India. You will never know how satisfying it has been to serve people in need.

45

I know now how important it is for me to finish college. And with God's help I intend to use my life to become a teacher and to help other people."

Bill was thinking about those words with which Jim closed his talk. It had been a good talk. Others had thought so, too. Sally, Jim's girl, had looked and smiled at Jim throughout the talk. Jim was bringing Sally over tonight. They had invited some of Jim's other friends, too, for pizza.

But the pizza party never came off. The Martens had begun to wonder why Jim and Sally and the others were not yet home when the phone rang, "Mr. Martens . . . . There's been an accident . . . . Can you hurry to City Hospital? They've taken Jim and Sally . . . ."

Later that night Bill sat alone, his head in his hands. Stunned. He couldn't believe it. Jim was dead. Sally might be crippled for life. There had been witnesses. A drunken driver had run a stoplight and hit Jim's car broadside. They never had a chance. "Why Jim and Sally?" Bill wondered. . . .

THE PROBLEM: WHY DO THE RIGHTEOUS SUFFER?

Unexplained evil in the world continues to be a roadblock to faith for many people. Some instances of suffering and hurt we can explain. There are errors of judgment and the sin and irresponsibility of men and nations. There are experiences of suffering we can blame on man's misuse of his freedom: the chain smoker who dies at age 55 from cancer of the lungs; the intoxicated teen-ager who roars through a school zone, killing an innocent 6-year-old; war, bringing death, terror, and homelessness to thousands.

But what about the man who is struck by a bolt of lightning? Or the tornadoes, hurricanes, flash floods, or earthquakes which kill and injure and leave many others homeless?

The problem for us is this: How can God, who is both almighty and all-loving, permit evil and suffering in His world? If He is almighty and still permits suffering, it would appear that His love is less than perfect. If He is all-loving and permits suffering, it would appear that His power is limited. So, the problem of evil is really the problem of trying to understand God.

Note that the problem of evil, or suffering, is a problem only to the man who believes in God. The man who has no faith in a Creator-God and does not believe in a guiding force must expect that this is the way things are. A handful of matches dropped on the table will fall helter-skelter. You don't expect a purposeful design. So, the problem of evil is really the problem of trying to understand God.

SOME ANSWERS GIVEN

Attempts people have made to explain evil include the following:

1. There are two Gods: one whose purposes are good and one whose purposes are evil. This was the solution offered by Zoroastrianism, a Persian religion centuries ago.

2. There is one God, but He permits a created and rebellious creature (the devil) to operate in and affect the world. But this view has sometimes pushed the responsibility for evil back on God!

3. Freedom exists not only in man but in all of nature. And something has gone wrong in the physical universe so that *the whole creation has been groaning in travail together until now* (Rom. 8:22).

4. There is one God, but His motives are a mixture of good and evil, as in the case of men.

5. There is an all-powerful God who has predestined certain people to be elected to salvation and others to eternal punishment. Everything that happens is by God's decree. According to this view, God is all-powerful but not all-good.

6. There is one God, and He is good; but He is not all-powerful. This view implies that God's intention is good, but He is not quite on top of things.

7. There is one God. He is all-powerful and basically good, but He brings evil upon us to punish us. Read John 9:1-3 or Luke 13:1-5 to see how Jesus refuted this explanation.

8. There is one God. He is all-powerful and basically good, but He deliberately brings evil upon us to test us and to develop faith

and trust in Him. The biblical basis for this idea is found in Hebrews 12:5, 6: *For the Lord disciplines him whom he loves. . . .*

The fact that so many answers have been proposed may be saying to us that the problem of evil cannot be explained logically. Not one of the above provides a wholly adequate, convincing answer.

THE BIBLE AND THE PROBLEM OF EVIL

In the Old Testament, the entire Book of Job deals with this problem. Job, the head of a tribal family, was an upright, God-fearing man. Through the years, things had been coming his way. He had a fine family of seven sons and three daughters. He had accumulated a lot of land, camels, cattle, and sheep.

Then one day the roof caved in on Job. Through a series of catastrophes, his possessions were suddenly wiped out, the family was gone, and even Job's health broke. Now Job's friends came to tell him that these misfortunes were a punishment for sin. But Job maintained that he had not sinned to merit such punishment!

Elihu suggested that Job's sufferings were a divine discipline of love to keep Job from sinning in the future. But this answer, too, Job rejected. Almost in despair and arrogance, Job had been crying out—where is God's justice? And then Job was confronted by a display of God's power (chapters 38-41). God began by questioning Job. *"Where were you when I laid the foundation of the earth?"* (Job 38:4). In this encounter with the God of all creation, Job suddenly glimpsed the greatness of God. How can Job, who is only a small part of God's creation, presume to pass judgment on the Creator? How can the creature expect to know all that is known to the Creator? And Job confesses:

"I know that thou canst do all things,
and that no purpose of thine can be thwarted. . . .
Therefore I have uttered what I did not understand,
things too wonderful for me. . . .
I had heard of thee by the hearing of the ear,
but now my eye sees thee;

therefore I despise myself,
   and repent in dust and ashes" (Job 42:2-6).

What made the difference to Job was not that God won an argument, but that God became real for him. He could now trust God for everything. There is no need for a logical answer to his problem. What matters is that the God who can "do all things" is also Job's God.

A passage in the New Testament that speaks of this problem is Romans 8:18-39. Here, also, there is no neat intellectual answer to the problem of evil. But Paul is writing about the resources available to help us meet experiences of suffering.

Read this passage in your Bible noting:
1. What Paul has to say about present sufferings (v. 18).
2. What resource has been given the Christian (vv. 26, 27).
3. The evidence God has given of His concern for us (vv. 28-34).
4. In a sentence, sum up the claim that is made in verses 35-39.

The Christian belief does not offer an intellectual answer to the problem of evil. It offers a religious answer—a faith which enables us to endure hardship in a spirit of triumph, to work against evil to reduce suffering, and to work for reconciliation in the world. There are answers we have to live out, not spell out. Christians believe that nothing, finally, will be able to separate us from God's love which we know in Christ.

We can be assured that God does not thoughtlessly or heartlessly inflict pain or misfortune on us. We can only believe that God is good and that some day He will make plain what we do not now understand. Meanwhile we seek to permit God to work with us even in painful experiences, looking for the good that can come out of what appear to be tragic situations. For *we know that in everything God works for good with those who love him . . .* (Rom. 8:28).

THE EVIL ONE

Following His baptism, Jesus spent forty days in the wilderness, tempted by Satan (Mk. 1:13). Vivid descriptions of this experience are given in Matthew 4:1-11 and Luke 4:1-13. Here the devil or

Satan is identified as the power of evil attempting to sidetrack Jesus from His God-given work.

It was the belief that Satan had at one time been one of God's servants, but that he had turned against God and was opposing all that was good. In the Book of Job, Satan was one of God's messengers whose responsibility was that of testing the goodness of men.

In the earlier writings of the Old Testament, the words *the devil* or *Satan* are not found, though the work of evil is evident. (Note 1 Kings 22:19-23.) But in the time of the later prophets, when the terrible experiences of the Exile affected the Hebrews, the word *Satan* began to appear in the writings. Satan means "adversary" or "accuser." In Hebrew thought Satan came to be the leader of the forces that were opposed to God and His goodness. In every way possible Satan tempted men to turn away from God, to be disobedient unto Him, and to enter into sin.

In New Testament times people firmly believed in harmful spirits. Jesus spoke of the power of the evil one (Mt. 13:19), Satan (Mt. 12:26), or the devil (Jn. 8:44). In later New Testament writings, especially the Revelation of John, there are other references to this power of evil working against God, and by which the people of God are deceived. Satan is here also identified with the serpent of Genesis 3 (Rev. 12:9; 20:2).

But in spite of all the development of the belief in the power of Satan, God always had the last word. Satan was never as powerful as God. While Satan seemed at times to be in control on earth and among men, while evil may have seemed to be too powerful to be overthrown, God would at the last destroy Satan and all his forces.

In the Middle Ages, a vivid belief in the devil persisted. In fact, the devil seemed to be everywhere! Popular writers described his exciting feats, how he appeared in meetings of witches as a big black tomcat or as a dog or some other creature. He seemed especially real to monks and nuns in monasteries. Martin Luther told how on one occasion the devil debated with him on the proper translation of a Scripture passage. Luther hurled his inkstand at him. It is alleged that the mark can still be seen on the wall of Luther's cell in Wartburg! Among the writers who contributed to a vivid picture of the devil and his work are Dante (*The Divine Comedy*) and John Milton (*Paradise Lost*).

SUGGESTIONS FOR OUR UNDERSTANDING OF THE DEVIL

1. Recognize first of all that the popular caricatures, such as the devil being a red creature with horns, tail, and pitchfork, spring from the superstition of medieval times. The power of evil is *much more* subtle and enticing.

2. This personal evil force called "the devil" works against God in the inner life of men and in the accumulated errors and prejudices of society. So the man or nation whose life is dominated by pride can become the incarnation of evil.

3. We dare not think of the devil as having existence other than as a created being. He is not an equal with God.

4. The Bible's interest is not so much to describe the devil as it is to point up the decisive victory Jesus Christ has won! The Bible is concerned with the resources that are available to deal with the deceitful wiles of the evil one.

5. Whatever emphasis the New Testament places on the devil as tempter, it never loses sight of the fact that man is responsible for his sin.

WORDS TO REMEMBER

Evil. 1) The unexplainable tragic events in nature or human life. 2) Moral evil, that which is contrary to divine law. 3) The power in the world that works against God.

The devil or Satan. Names given to the spirit or power of evil at work against God.

HOW DO YOU FEEL ABOUT THIS?

1. When a school bus plunged over a bridge railing and seventeen children drowned in the icy waters, a teen-ager wrote these reflections. "Perhaps God did this so older people would take notice and realize God was still around. Perhaps by making all

these children drown, He was trying to get people to see that He was more powerful than they. Maybe God thought the world was getting too confusing and that there was too much fighting of wars and too much hate in the world for these poor innocent children to live with; so He took them out of this mad, messy world. God can take any age of people, young or old."

In what way do you agree or disagree with this view of God? What is inadequate about this understanding of God? What truths about God are expressed here?

2. What positive values can come out of experiences of suffering? Can you think of examples?

3. The baptismal service form includes the question: "Do you in the presence of God and this assembly, solemnly renounce the devil and all his works, and declare the Lord to be your God?" What does this mean to you?

A PRAYER

God grant me the serenity to accept things I cannot change, courage to change things I can, and wisdom to know the difference.

Why did it happen?

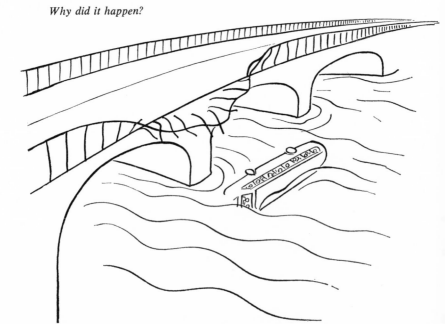

Chapter 8

Man in Revolt

Genesis 1:26, 27; 3:1-7; Psalm 8; Romans 3:9-18, 23

The Bible is the truest record of how God shows himself; it tells us what He is like; it describes His acts in the lives of people and nations; it tells of His mighty acts in creation and in providing for His world. God is the central character of this story.

But the Bible has also to do with us. Here is the account of how God kept telling men who they were, from where they had come, where they were going, what they were destined to be, how they should live with one another, and how they ought to respond to His gracious dealings with them.

But we find it hard to play second fiddle. We like to come in first. And so the Bible's story includes our attempts to muscle in on God, to push Him offstage so that we can hog the spotlight. This tendency to reject our Creator and to miss becoming what God meant us to be we must now try to understand if we hope to find out who we really are.

WHO AM I?

Plato defined man as "a two-legged animal without feathers." But when Diogenes exhibited a plucked hen in the marketplace and called it "Plato's man" this definition seemed a bit inadequate!

Who am I? There have been many attempts to understand the meaning of our being here. Common sense says that man is a person. He is a person in that he differs from animals and things because he can make and use tools, language, and create complex cultures. Man talks, thinks, laughs, feels, prays, and strives for the improvement of his personality.

Science tells us that man is a complicated animal. The sciences see man as a physical creature, an organism made up of millions of cells, as so much energy.

Philosophers, who make use of reason and the description of the sciences, try to view man with the whole world as the context. Their answer: "Man is a sample of the universe."

Still others contend there is a religious dimension to life. And from the standpoint of religion, man is "a servant of superior values."[14]

Who am I? A community of millions of cells living together? An animal? A complex person? A sample of the universe? A servant of superior values? In a sense I am all of these, but. . . .

A PESSIMISTIC VIEW

In man's search for meaning, a pessimistic view has dominated the centuries. It is based upon man's behavior. An old Chinese proverb says, "All the people are your relatives; expect therefore trouble from them." The philosopher, Schopenhauer, likened mankind to a herd of porcupine huddling together to keep warm. If they draw too close, they prick each other painfully with their needles; if they separate too far, they freeze.

It was this observation of how people behave toward each other that prompted Bernard Shaw to say, "Man is the only animal of which I am thoroughly and cravenly afraid. I have never thought much of the courage of a lion tamer. Inside the cage he is at least safe from other men. There is less harm in a well-fed lion. It has no class: in short, no reason for destroying anything it does not want to eat."[15]

There are about 3 billion of us strange creatures. We can do marvelous things . . .

Design supersonic jets that can take us anyplace on earth in a matter of hours.

Provide instant communication so that we can see and hear what happens anywhere when it happens.

Produce music like Haydn's *Creation,* or paintings such as

Da Vinci's *The Last Supper,* and literature like the plays of William Shakespeare.

Wipe out crippling polio, and restore sight through corneal transplants.

Build machines that do much of the backbreaking work, and machines that even calculate and think for us.

Build children's homes and retirement centers because we believe in the worth of each person.

But every now and then we also turn our best brains, our factories and manpower, to the task of killing each other. We destroy the cities we have built.

By 1900 there had been some reasons for optimism. Men had conquered and spanned the continent. Railroads and telephones and electricity were a reality. The previously unbelievable dreams of horseless carriages and men flying through the air were becoming real. With advances in education and self-understanding, man was finally coming of age! The Golden Age seemed just around the corner!

But the bubble of optimism was punctured by World War I (1914-1918), the Russian communist revolution (1917-1921). Then followed Hitler and Auschwitz (1933-1944). The Japanese attack on Pearl Harbor (1941), the American A-bombs on Hiroshima and Nagasaki (1945), and a long list of other bloody conflicts like Korea, Congo, and Vietnam.

But not only do worldwide conflicts worry us. Within our own lives we feel something of a war going on. We make good resolutions and break them. We are a puzzle and a worry to ourselves. The Apostle Paul summed up the problem for us all, *For I do not do the good I want, but the evil I do not want is what I do . . . Wretched man that I am! Who will deliver me from this body of death?* (Rom. 7:19, 24).

THE CHRISTIAN POINT OF VIEW

The Christian faith does not permit us to settle for the pessimistic view of man. Neither do we take stock in a false optimism.

But the Christian view is at the same time a low view and a high view of man.

1. We have been created *in the image of God* (Gen. 1:27). We have been created for dominion, for working with God in His world. That God should concern himself about us, and make us *little less than God* is the amazing truth that absorbs the thought of the writer of Psalm 8.

2. At the same time, the Bible recognizes that something has happened, and continues to happen, to keep us from fulfilling God's plan for us. *All have sinned and fall short of the glory of God* (Rom. 3:23) is Paul's statement of the situation.

One of the Bible's stories to explain sin is found in Genesis 3. The Adam and Eve story is really the story of all mankind, people wanting to be as gods, and overstepping the limits that God has placed upon them. Read Genesis 3:1-7. Note especially phrases in verses 5 and 6 that may be clues to what our sin really is. And remember, all of us are involved in this, desiring to be more than we can ever be, thus marring "the image," breaking fellowship with the One who is our Creator.

3. But the story of man does not end there, says the Christian faith. *For God so loved the world* [and rebellious man] *that he gave his only Son, that whoever believes in him should not perish, but have eternal life* (Jn. 3:16).

It is the claim of the Christian faith that through Jesus Christ God has provided a way for us to be reconciled to Him. And thus it is the claim of Christian faith that man's highest destiny is to be a son of God. We are not our true selves until we are God's. *So through God you are no longer a slave but a son, and if a son then an heir* (Gal. 4:7).

A DIAGNOSIS OF THE PROBLEM: SIN AND SINS

You are sick. You've missed two days of school. Your head aches and your eyes hurt. Now you discover that you have a fever —102.4 degrees. You decide it's time to see the doctor. The doctor tells you, "You're a sick fellow. You are not meant to have a headache and fever like that. You really ought to be well. That's

56

Something is wrong here, but what?

what you were intended for." But this is not why you came. This much you already know. You want the doctor to get down to the bottom of it and find out what really is ailing you. After all, you already know that aspirin will reduce the fever and relieve your aching head. But you want to knock out whatever it is that leaves you weak and helpless.

"That coach makes me sick with his talk about teamwork. I know the score better than that. No one watches the guys who throw the passes. It's the one who makes the baskets who's the star. And I intend to be number one!"

Jane took the box from the closet shelf. Once more she looked at the loot—a bracelet, three sets of earrings, a couple of paperbacks, cologne, and cigarettes. It didn't mean much really. But why was she uneasy? Nobody caught her. Turn it back? What difference would this little bit of stuff make? Maybe the gang would soon lay off this shoplifting spree. . . .

Headings from the morning paper: Police Hunt Arsonist . . . Tension Mounts in Middle East . . . Girl Slain in Apartment . . . Score Hurt in Campus Riot . . .

Something is wrong here. But what? Is this sin? Or are the sorry stories we read about in the paper, or hear on the evening newscast the symptoms of sin?

57

The Pharisees, a group of religious people in Jesus' day, had sin figured out, they thought. Sin, as far as they were concerned, was disobeying the law. And they had quite a list: laws about how far you could walk on the Sabbath, what you could or could not eat, laws about whom you could associate with, laws about tithing garden seeds! They had so many laws that it was a full-time job just to keep informed. Consequently, the mass of the working people they simply called "sinners," because ignorantly, if not deliberately, they would break some of the laws all the time.

But Jesus told the Pharisees that they had become so concerned about the symptoms, that they failed to recognize what sin is all about. Not the acts of a person, but man's evil heart that leads him to these acts, needs primary attention (Mk. 7:15). Jesus was saying: There is a difference between sin (that attitude which separates one from God) and sins (those actions which a person commits). It is not the committing of sins that makes a person sinful, but rather, the other way around. A person commits sins because he has already separated himself from God.

Sin is a condition within us which causes us to miss the mark. Jesus' definition of sin can be found in Mark 8:35: *Whoever would save his life will lose it.* Sin is a misplaced love of self. It is self-sufficiency insisting on my own way and daring to believe that I can reach my self-chosen goals in my own strength. For an example of this, read the story in Mark 10:17-27.

Centuries of Christian experience have confirmed that of all sins, pride—the love of self—is the root sin. Pride is man insisting that he is sovereign. It is man insisting on his own way, man claiming to be pilot of his own ship. Pride is a "swelling of the heart." Man playing God.

Now read Genesis 3:1-7 again. Note how the tempter appeals to Eve's self-centeredness.

WHAT ABOUT "ORIGINAL SIN"?

Sin always involves freedom and choice. To be human is not sin. We cannot help that. But the doctrine of original sin refers to this dominant tendency in every person to assert his will against God instead of toward or for God.

Our problem is that as infants we come to see the world stretching around us. We are in the middle of it. The things that hurt us, we call bad. The things that please us, we call good. Our standard of value is the way things affect us.

"Each of us takes his place in the center of his own world," says William Temple. "But I am not the center of the world, or the standard of reference as between good and bad; I am not, and God is. In other words, from the beginning I put myself in God's place. This is my original sin. I was doing it before I could speak, and everyone else has been doing it from early infancy. I am not "guilty" on this account because I could not help it. But I am in a state, from birth, in which I shall bring disaster on myself and everyone affected by my conduct unless I can escape from it."[16]

All have sinned and fall short of the glory of God (Rom. 3:23) is Paul's statement of the situation. But we cannot hide behind the idea of the disobedience of the first two people bringing punishment on the whole human race. Genesis 3 must be read in the light of the Bible's other passages that emphasize each individual's responsibility before God. Even Paul's references to *one man's trespass* (Rom. 5:12, 15, 17, 18) must be read in the light of each person's responsibility. The emphasis here is on the fact that *all have sinned.*

So also, Psalm 51:5, *in sin did my mother conceive me* does not mean that we are sinners because of the act of our parents in bringing us into the world. The point of Psalm 51:5 is: *"Like the rest of men, I have been a sinner from birth."*

And to be delivered from this situation we need help—help that can come only from beyond ourselves.

QUESTIONS TO CONSIDER

1. Why has a pessimistic view dominated centuries of thought about man? What evidence warns against being too optimistic in our view of man?

2. Why do we speak of the Christian faith as giving us both a low view and high view of man?

3. What is the difference between "sins" and SIN? What example can you suggest? What happens when we try to work only with "sins"? Can we deal with SIN without also eliminating the "sins"?

4. When the Japanese Christian, Toyohiko Kagawa, was asked, "What is the first thing in knowing the will of God?" he replied, "Surrender." What do you think he meant by that?

14. Robert L. Calhoun, *What Is Man?* (Hazen Books edition; New York: Association Press, 1953), p. 59.

15. Gerald Kennedy, *A Reader's Notebook* (New York: Harper and Brothers, 1953), p. 172.

16. William Temple, *Christianity and Social Order* (London: Penguin, 1942), pp. 37, 38.

Chapter 9

When We Miss the Mark

"When you were dead in your sins and trespasses, those sins and trespasses in which you once walked, living life in the way this present age lives it, living life as the ruler of the power of the air dictates it, that spirit which now operates in the children of disobedience—and once all we too lived the same kind of life as these children of disobedience do, a life in which we were at the mercy of the desires of our lower nature and of our own designs, a life in which, as far as human nature goes, we deserved nothing but the wrath of God. . . ."[17]

MISSING THE MARK

This was Tom's first try at archery. As he pulled back on the bowstring and released it, the arrow sailed off, landing five yards to the right of the target. But with a little practice, Tom found the range and finally was able to put the arrow right through the bulls-eye.

But even if Tom were to practice every day, and were to become an accomplished archer, and could regularly hit the bullseye, he would likely not hit it every time. Even for the best archer, the arrow sometimes strays. An unexpected gust of wind, a defective arrow, a frayed bowstring, a fatigued or tense body, a lapse in concentration—one or a dozen things can go wrong. The arrow goes off course and misses the mark.

To miss the mark is the literal meaning of one of the Bible's words for sin. No one hits the bulls-eye all of the time. None of us lives up to the full intention God has for our life. We fall short. We veer off course. We miss the mark. This is the human situation. The evidence is plain. Man is a sinner.

61

Today we look at the result of sin. Again we look at Genesis 3 to see what happens when we sin. In the previous session we noted how Genesis 3:6, 7 gave us a clue to the nature of sin. Sin is misplaced self-love, the refusal to accept our place as creature. Instead of acknowledging the Creator, we try to move into His place.

Note: In Genesis 3:1-7 we can see how subtly the temptation to sin comes. Not by way of a horrible creature with horns and tail, nor even an ugly snake! Oh no, we wouldn't have anything to do with sin then! So often, instead, temptation comes through the things that are good and attractive. And then comes the thought that maybe God need not be taken so seriously. This one little thing, this one little act, or thought, surely won't make that much difference!

What happens when we sin? Read through Genesis 3 again and list all of the results of sin that you can find.

GUILT

The lie detector used by law-enforcement officers is based on the knowledge that lying is often accompanied by bodily reactions. Increased heartbeat, sweating, flushing, swallowing, and other emotional reactions often accompany conscious deceptions. We cannot be what we are not without effects upon our life. For we are answerable for our life. Guilt is one of the most serious results of sin. For guilt enslaves us so that we are no longer free to act as children of God.

Let us look at several obvious results of guilt in the story of Adam and Eve.

1. *The Involvement of Others . . . She also gave some to her husband, and he ate* (v. 6). Suddenly it was too frightening to walk about alone in the garden with the forbidden fruit. So Eve sought an accomplice.

Sin causes separation from God and always isolates us. And in one way or another I must live in fellowship with others. If I am corrupt, then others must be corrupt, too. At least it won't seem so bad if others are involved!

"Well, Bill did it, too!" Have you ever heard that kind of remark? Or caught yourself saying it?

2. *Fear—Running—Hiding* (vv. 7, 8). Now comes the recognition that one's life is suddenly open to God, and to others! The God who a moment before seemed a God not to be taken too seriously becomes a terror to us!

Arnie was a fugitive. He had stolen money belonging to a firm in which he had been a trusted bookkeeper. Several hundred dollars, taken over a period of six months, had been successfully concealed until a company auditor uncovered clues that Arnie knew would lead him to the truth. Rather than face the truth and the disgrace he was sure would ruin his reputation and wreck his family, he boarded a train. He would lose himself in a strange city, where no one knew him.

What Arnie didn't know was that his employer would permit him to continue his job and repay the money. And his family was willing to forgive him. His guilt compelled him to run away, rather than to reckon with these possibilities.

A young man wrote his pastor: "I have disobeyed God and tried to get by with it. I'm finding out the hard way that God is not mocked and whatsoever a man sows, he shall reap. . . . Sometimes I become fearful of what God will do with me and how He will expose me. It is so hard to try to break the habit of running away from God. . . ."

God's *"Where are you?"* keeps ringing in our ears when we sin.

3. *Making Excuses* (vv. 9-13). Another result of sin and guilt is that great game of "passing the buck." The dialogue between God and Adam and Eve goes like this:

God: "Where are you?"

Adam: "I was afraid, because I was naked; and I hid myself." (That's not really why they hid. Not modesty, but the sudden recognition that their lives were bared before God. What they really were was now plain.)

God: "Who told you . . . Have you eaten of the tree . . . ?"

Adam: "The woman whom thou gavest to be with me. . . ."

Does any of this sound familiar?

(Get that? the woman whom *thou gavest me!* Not Adam, not even Eve, but now it's God's fault!)

Now it is Eve's turn:

God: "What is this that you have done?"

Eve: "I didn't start this either, dear heavenly Father. It was the serpent whom Thou didst put in paradise. He started the whole thing." (Now it's the devil's fault. And finally, really God's fault. For He made us to begin with. And He put the tree there in such a tempting place!) [18]

Does any of this sound familiar? Guilt keeps us from an honest look at our own responsibility.

4. *Separation—Alienation—Aloneness*

Read Genesis 3:17-19 and 22-24. The man and woman are turned from the Garden. Paradise is lost. By disobedience to their Creator, the man and woman have put themselves out of the relationship they had enjoyed. Something good has been broken, something that the man will never be able to restore.

Sin damages any relationship of trust, whether between people, or between man and God. And when we cannot trust, we become fearful, isolated from each other, and alone. This is hell—to be cut off from God and from others.

(Note: Sometimes Genesis 3:17-19 is used to teach that work is a curse. But we do not get the Christian "doctrine of work" from this passage. This will be discussed in Lesson 24.)

5. *Death. "You shall not eat of the fruit . . . , lest you die* (Gen. 3:3). Paul, writing to the Romans, says: *Therefore as sin came into the world through one man and death through sin,*

64

and so death spread to all men because all men sinned . . . (Rom. 5:12). Or again, *the wages of sin is death* . . . (Rom. 6:23).

The Bible recognizes that all men die. And death cannot be simply reduced to a process of nature. Human life is always lived under the shadow of death, a reminder that we are mortal beings, and not gods.

But there is another sense in which we must think of death. One day Jesus said to His disciples, *Do not fear those who kill the body, and after that have no more that they can do . . . fear him who, after he has killed, has power to cast into hell; yes, I tell you, fear him!* (Lk. 12:4, 5).

There is something worse than death of the body. That is the death due to sin, a drying up of the spirit, Christless living and dying. It is this result of sin that we must now reckon with.

THE KILLING EFFECTS OF SIN

The Letter to the Ephesians has these words: *When you were dead through the trespasses and sins in which you once walked . . .* (Eph. 2:1, 2).

William Barclay points out how sin always has a killing effect in his commentary on Galatians and Ephesians. Sin kills *innocence*. No one is precisely the same after he has sinned. If a new car has had a fender smashed, we can get the dent taken care of and new paint put on, but it is never again quite the same car. So sin kills innocence.

Sin kills *ideals*. Each sin makes the next sin easier. Men begin to do without a qualm the thing which once they regarded with horror.

Sin kills the *will*. When we allow some habit, some indulgence, some secret or forbidden practice to master us, we become its slave. The thing so grips us that we cannot break its grip.

When the selfishness of sin dominates our life, we tend to die to the purposes God has for us. Paul uses the term, *slaves of sin* (Rom. 6:20). This means being a slave to oneself. When we become devoted to the job of satisfying ourselves, we are in real trouble.

Paul is describing the ancient Greek and Roman world in Romans 1:18-32. The depersonalizing of masses of people in slavery, cruelty, sensuality, love of amusement, were all part of this world. This ancient civilization, for all its greatness, was decaying on the inside. The claim of the Creator God was being ignored. Men gloried in human wisdom, material strength, and desires of the body. And so Paul observes:

God gave them up in the lusts of their hearts. . . .
God gave them up to dishonorable passions. . . .
God . . . has given them up to their own depraved reason . . .
(Rom. 1:24, 26, 28, NEB).

What is there in your teen-world, in the society or community in which you live that resembles the kind of world of which Paul speaks? Do you know fellows or girls who are "dead" to God and slaves to themselves? Are there areas in your life where "life with God" has been crowded out by other things of greater interest to you?

It is the New Testament's claim and the church's belief that in Jesus Christ and only in Jesus Christ can we die to sin, and be made alive unto God. Not only is this possible, but that this is God's purpose for every man is the theme of the Bible: *He who has the Son has life; he who has not the Son of God has not life* (1 Jn.: 5:12).

FOR YOU TO THINK ABOUT AND DO

1. Even though we believe God can forgive, are there some wrongs that can never be restored and made right? What, for example?

2. Read Psalm 51 or Psalm 32 as a confession of sin and prayer for forgiveness.

3. Observe the following facts about these prominent figures in the Bible's story:

Jacob deceived his father and tricked his brother.

Moses killed a man.

David took another's wife.

Peter battled a fiery temper, on an impulse cut off a man's ear, and denied his Lord three times.

Saul of Tarsus caused havoc in the early church by imprisoning Christians.

But note that in spite of these failures, these men are permitted to rise up, so that sin did not leave them immobilized. What is the secret?

4. Have you come to grips with the selfishness and the pride in your life that stands between you and God? To confess your failures to God, or to some person you trust, may be the first step in finding help.

5. Think about this prayer from George Matheson's hymn:
"Make me a captive, Lord,
And then I shall be free."

6. If death is related to sin and if death came into the world because of sin as Romans 5:12 and Romans 6:23 suggest, what does Jesus' comment in Luke 13:1-5 add to our understanding about a particular death?

17. William Barclay, *The Letters to the Galatians and Ephesians* (Philadelphia: Westminster Press, 1956), p. 111.
18. Helmut Thielicke, *How the World Began* (Philadelphia: Fortress Press, 1961), pp. 161, 162.

Chapter 10

God's Answer to Sin

For all the promises of God find their Yes in him.

2 Corinthians 1:20

PROMISES AND MY LIFE

We live by promises. "I'll meet you at the drive-in at 7:30," is a promise to be there. A check is a promise that there is money in the bank to cover the purchase. Taking a job is a promise to be there on time and to do what the employer requires.

There is freedom and security in the firm mutual commitments by which we live. Your parents' marriage vows, the contract for purchase of the house in which you live, the treaties between this and other nations make your life relatively secure and free. Imagine life without these and the many other binding promises.

But promises are not always kept. Perhaps that is why we find it hard to think of a promise about which there is no doubt. One of the Bible's greatest themes is God's promise to deliver men from the curse of sin, to welcome men back as children of God after any and every rebellious act. The Christian gospel is the good news that God will never walk out on man. This is what the title of the two parts of the Bible is all about: Old Covenant—New Covenant. It's all about God's love which stays with every sinner to the end unless the sinner tears himself out of the arms of God.

This understanding of how God deals with human sin is unique. In non-Christian religions men may look upon their gods as preoccupied or disinterested or limited. So they need to attract their god's attention, or beg him, or acquire a specialized knowledge of him. But no, says the Christian faith, God has already taken the first step for our salvation long ago.

The Bible writers speak of it as a promise—a promise fulfilled. Had Jesus never come, we might have doubted this tremendous promise of God as being too good to be true. But God loves us so much that He gave us His son . . . "Jesus is the Yes to every promise of God," writes Paul to the Christians at Corinth (2 Cor. 1:20).

It is this promise of salvation we study today, noting that God's answer to sin is not an afterthought, but part of a divine plan. This plan includes all men living in every age. It includes you and me.

THE PROBLEM

The early chapters of Genesis tell of the creation. Here we read that God made the world, that He made everything in it. But it is our story, too. He made you and me so that we can take our place in this world and care for it.

But God has made us free to choose. The third chapter of Genesis records the story of Adam and Eve who chose to disobey God and go their own way. To their disappointment, they discovered they could no longer live as members of God's family. We read that story knowing that it really is about any of us.

Then in the pages of the Book of Genesis come other stories about men who chose to disobey God. In doing so they became divided from each other and lived in fear and hatred . . .

> Cain and Abel (chap. 4)
> People in the days of Noah (chaps. 6-9)
> Building the tower of Babel (chap. 11)

But God was not willing to let men defeat His plan and purpose. From the very beginning the Bible lets us know that God is a speaking God. Note how the theme "and God said" recurs over and over in Genesis 1. God's universe is one of community and communication, both of which man is constantly breaking, and God is restoring. From Genesis chapter 11 onward is the story of God's attempt to reconstruct the world by preparing a people through whom He could lead man back into fellowship with himself.

69

THE PROMISE

God's plan included choosing a man, a family, and nation. The man was Abraham, the family and nation the Hebrews. Something happened in the life of Abraham. Whether it was sudden or the result of a long contemplation on true religion, we do not know. But it became a turning point for Abraham, and the whole of human history.

Abraham became deeply aware of God. He felt God was calling him to live by faith and to begin a journey. He believed God would lead him.

Genesis 12:1-3 is the story of that call and promise. This promise of a nation through whom all the nations of the world would be blessed is repeated to Isaac (Gen. 26:3), Jacob (Gen. 28:13, 14), and linked to God's later call of Moses to lead His people from Egypt toward the promised land (Gen. 50:22-25; Ex. 12:25).

Even after the people were settled in the land of promise, the conviction grew that God was using them for a special purpose. In the time of King David, 1000 B.C., when the nation had become strong this promise appeared to be fulfilled (2 Kings 7:12, 16, 18-29).

Later, when civil war divided the kingdom (922 B.C.) and Jerusalem was attacked and the temple destroyed (586 B.C.), and Exile to a foreign land became the lot of many of the Hebrews, God's promise was put before the people again. The prophets and a remnant of the people continued their hope that God would give to His people a new kingdom, and a new king (Jer. 23:5; Ezek. 37: 24, 25).

After the time of Exile, when many Hebrews returned to Jerusalem and rebuilt the temple, the promise of God came to be linked clearly with a coming Messiah. This servant of God is described in the prophecies in Isaiah, chapters 49-57.

THE COVENANT

The history of the Hebrews may not have been so different from that of other people. Events took place in their midst in much the same way as they did among other peoples. Yet, there was a difference. Among the Hebrews there were men who saw in the events of nature and history the movements of a divine hand. There were priests and prophets saying that there was a purpose in all these things that happened. That God would bless the people of Israel and make of them a great nation was not because they were so good. The Book of Deuteronomy (chap. 7) says, No, not that! But simply because God loved Israel, He chose it. And the calling was not first of all for Israel's own sake, but for the sake of the world. It was because of God's purpose!

The prophets speak of God's purpose for the Hebrews as a covenant. God entered into a covenant, an agreement with Abraham, the man from Ur of the Chaldees. This covenant was then extended to Abraham's descendants. Each was responsible to the other for certain obligations. Abraham and the Hebrews were to live by faith and to follow God's leading. God would provide them with a land and the awareness of the presence of a faithful and righteous God.

The Hebrews came to look upon the Law, as it was given to Moses, as a guide for their side of the covenant relation to God. These commandments, written on stone, served the Hebrews as a means of separation from the world and as a guide for their God-given purpose.

But the people discovered that they were falling short and failing to realize God's full promise in their daily lives.

By Jeremiah's time, a new covenant was already being prophesied (Jer. 31:31-34). The days will come, said Jeremiah, when God's Law will no longer be written on stone, but be written into the hearts of all believers.

THE PROMISE FULFILLED

God's promise holds a central place in the New Testament. The writers of the New Testament, men who had lived with Jesus and with those who knew Jesus most intimately, searched their Scriptures (the Old Testament). Here they found many signs, pointers, prophecies, that they had now seen fulfilled in Jesus' own life. They saw in Jesus the fullfillment of God's promise of salvation.

1. *Jesus' own words about His work* (Lk. 4:16-21).

At the beginning of Jesus' ministry, when He was invited to speak in His hometown synagogue, Jesus chose to read the words from Isaiah 61:1, 2. *"The Spirit of the Lord is upon me, because he has anointed me. . . .* Then He closed the book and said: *"Today this scripture has been fulfilled in your hearing."* Here—and later—in His words and acts, He clearly identified himself with God's promise of salvation now come true in Him.

2. *Peter's message at Pentecost* (Acts 2).

Fifty days after Jesus' death and resurrection, Peter and the other disciples were together in a room in Jerusalem. Earlier one hundred and twenty other disciples were mentioned (Acts 1:15). These and other Jewish people were present when an incredible thing happened. The disciples spoke in strange sounds. A crowd gathered quickly. What was going on here?

Peter, the spokesman, explained quickly. "These men are not drunk. It's too early in the day for that!" No indeed—this is the pouring out of God's Spirit! "This is the Word of God coming true before your eyes," said Peter. "This Jesus—who was killed, and whom we saw raised up—is the fulfillment of God's promise!"

If you scan Peter's message, recorded in Acts 2:14-39, you will note that Peter uses at least four quotations from the Old Testament Scriptures to back up his message.

3. *Paul's understanding of Jesus.* The Apostle Paul, that great early proclaimer of the Christian faith, was convinced that it is in Jesus Christ that God's promises receive their perfect fulfillment. His sermons recorded in Acts declare it: *God has brought to Israel a Savior, Jesus, as he promised* (Acts 13:23, 32, 33). His writings proclaim it: *Christ became a servant to the circumcised to show God's truthfulness, in order to confirm the promises given to the patriarchs . . .* (Rom. 15:8), *that in Christ Jesus the blessing of Abraham might come upon the Gentiles, that we might receive the promise of the Spirit through faith* (Gal. 3:14).

And so Paul, who saw God's promise to Abraham being fulfilled in Jesus Christ—saw the Christian believer as being the recipient of this promise. Believers in Christ become the children of God (Rom. 9:8; Gal. 4:28). The church becomes the new Israel of God (Gal. 6:16). We are the heirs of the promises of God (Gal. 3:26-29).

The gospel, the good news that the church has to tell, consists in proclaiming that the promises formerly transmitted through the prophets are now fulfilled in the person of Jesus of Nazareth (Rom. 1:2, 3).

GOD'S PLAN—FOR WHOM?

Japan's Mount Fuji is an old volcano. Each summer thousands of tourists and pilgrims climb the well-beaten paths up the slopes. It has become the source of inspiration for many artists and poets. But Mount Fuji, and the other volcanic peaks and craters of Japan, have also become the "jumping-off place" for thousands of youth for whom life no longer seems tolerable. Disappointed lovers, students who have failed, youth for whom the problems of life have gotten too big, seek an "out" by jumping off into the darkness of an old volcanic crater.

Japan has 20,000 suicides a year, many of whom are young people. The United States, with a larger population, also has about 20,000 suicide deaths a year. Of these, 300 are teen-agers. But for every young person who takes his own life, fifty others attempt to do so. And the baffling fact is that the teen-ager may resort to suicide in dealing with seemingly trivial problems—because a beloved teacher bawls him out, his girl friend jilts him, or his pet dog is hit by a car.

When life seems hopeless . . . when we are absolutely positive that Mom or Dad will never understand us . . . when our best friend has let us down . . . or we have botched things and can't bear to face our failure . . . when our moods immobilize us . . . and we feel rejected, alone, desperate, Christ gives us hope!

People are really very much alike. Oh, there are differences, of course. Some are tall and thin, some short and fat. Some have brown eyes, some blue eyes, some blond hair, and some black hair. Some have fair skin, others dark skin. And our abilities dif-

People are really very much alike.

fer, either because of inheritance or learning. Our temperaments differ in the way we have become accustomed to react to life.

But basically we are alike in our need—the need to be accepted, to be loved, to see some purpose, some worth in our lives.

The Christian faith claims that Christ brings meaning into our lives. And the evidence of history is that His word has been of enduring importance to men, and His death has proved the uniqueness of its power in the experience of man. A sense of worth and purpose is made available through Christ for people living in every age, in every place. No one is outside the reach of Christ's act. No one.

For we are alike in our need. We are not complete until we know we belong to God. The answer to life lies not in our family name, the gang we run around with, the clothes we wear, the color of our skin, or the area in which we live. The answer lies in God's love, made real through Jesus Christ. Christ came for the beatnik rebel, the class valedictorian, the youth group president, the average kid, the whole range of persons we know. And that includes us.

IMPORTANT WORDS

> *Promise.* a vow; a pledge. God's intended purpose and His deeds to complete it can be seen as a "promise fulfilled."
>
> *Covenant.* Solemn agreement between two or more persons; agreement between God and men.
>
> *Salvation.* The saving of man from sin's consequences. Deliverance from sin through Christ's sacrifice of himself for men. Freedom from sin and fellowship with God.

FOR YOU TO THINK ABOUT

1. Write in your own words God's promise to His people as the Old and New Testaments present it.

2. What does this promise say to you about the work of the Christian church?

3. If God through His covenant reaches out to us for our salvation, and if Jesus Christ is *the only way,* why does not everyone accept God's offer in Christ?

4. Discuss this statement: "The purpose of God is to create a community, which, in all the detail of its life, will show the characteristics of the people of God, and thus make the true God known."

Chapter 11

Salvation and the Commandments

"You shall love the Lord your God with all your heart. . . . And . . . you shall love your neighbor as yourself.

Matthew 22:37, 39

THE PROBLEM OF BEING GOOD

That Laurel family! Why did we have to get mixed up with them anyway? Dad always said they were no good. I guess we should never have invited them to church. The nerve of Don, suggesting we have a dance at our next youth meeting! He only comes to Sunday school half the time anyway. Brags about how he'll enlist in the Air Force soon as he's old enough! Doesn't seem to care anything about living a Christian life. Sure he's a smooth talker . . . but I can't see what those girls see in him. . . .

Ever feel this way about someone you do not like, about someone who does not seem to measure up? Ever think of the Christian life as living by a set of rules—not dancing or going to movies, or not drinking or smoking?

Sometimes we may think, how simple it would be if we could pull a list of do's and don't's out of a desk drawer and find it all laid out for us. But the Christian life cannot be reduced to a set of rules.

In the Bible we read about a man who had kept all the rules— he thought. Read the story Jesus tells in Mark 10:17-22. From childhood this man had tried to be good. But being good was not enough. Obeying all the rules did not bring satisfaction. He was so concerned about keeping the rules in order to be right with

God that he missed sharing his life with others and helping others.

So we can easily worry ourselves sick about doing nothing wrong, and still miss what life is all about!

What's this? It doesn't make any difference how we act? Whether we are good or bad? No, that isn't what we are saying. But the problem of being good is that we can never be good enough. We may be good in comparison to another (whom we have carefully selected)! But whenever we compare ourselves by God's holy purposes for us, we know we fall desperately short.

What is the relationship of salvation and the commandments? of law and grace? The Bible has much to say on this topic.

THE TORAH—AND LOVE FOR THE LAW

Every Sabbath, in Jewish synagogues all over the world, an important ritual takes place. As the congregation stands in reverence, the curtain covering the Ark in the front wall of the synagogue is drawn open. The rabbi carefully lifts out a large scroll, called the Torah, and places it upon a special reading table. The Torah scroll is a handwritten copy in the Hebrew language of the first five books of the Old Testament. These first five books are also called the Pentateuch. Each Sabbath a specified portion of the Torah is read.

Throughout their history the Jews have treated the Torah with reverence and love. One custom, still observed by some Jews, is to introduce the child to his first religious instruction by placing a drop of honey on the first page of the Bible and asking the child to kiss it. God's law is shown to be sweet, and from his earliest years, the Jewish child is taught to love and respect it.[19]

Torah is the Hebrew word for law. The word appears 220 times in the Old Testament. To the Jews these first five books are especially sacred. They believe God gave these laws to them through Moses. God's very command is given through these words, they believe, as summed up in the central prayer of their worship, the *Shema*: *"Hear, O Israel: The Lord our God is one Lord; and you shall love the Lord your God with all your heart, and with all your soul, and with all your might* (Deut. 6:4).

77

For devout Jews the Law is not seen as a burden. It is cause for the highest joy. Here is part of God's promise. Here is proof of the special love and care which God has for His people. It was the Law that separated them from the world, that reminded them that they were "children of righteousness."

This explains the tone of Psalm 119, a long meditation on the blessings of God's law: *Oh, how I love thy law!* (v. 97).

DIFFERENT KINDS OF LAWS IN THE OLD TESTAMENT

What kinds of laws does the Bible contain? To whom were they given, and why?

The law codes found in the Old Testament may be placed into several groups.

1. *The Ten Commandments.* The two accounts of these are in Exodus 20:1-17 and Deuteronomy 5:6-21. These basic rules about man's relationship to God and to his fellowmen were given by God to the people, through Moses, at Mount Sinai at the time of the exodus from Egypt.

2. *The terms of God's covenant with Israel.* Exodus 20:22— 23:19 gives a set of additional specific commands to regulate the life of the early Israelite community. Another version is found in Exodus 34:10-16. Some scholars think this is an earlier form of the command.

3. *The Code of Deuteronomy.* Deuteronomy means second law. This book was written as a series of addresses delivered by Moses to the children of Israel before their entrance into the promised land. It is a call to remember the God who had led them, and to obey His commands.

The story of a great reform in 621 B.C. is found in 2 Kings 22— 23. As workmen were repairing the temple, a law book was found and taken to King Josiah. When the book was read to him, he was so moved that he tore his clothes, called the people together, and had the book read to them. This was the beginning of a great religious reform.

This book of the law found in the temple was in all probability Deuteronomy, or some portion of it. It is likely that the core

Those laws!

of the present book was very old, but that it was expanded and edited by pupils of the eighth century prophets.

4. *Code of Holiness.* Leviticus, chapters 17-27, contains ancient laws governing the religious life of the Hebrew people.

5. *The priestly legislation.* The early chapters of Leviticus deal with the system of sacrifice, and provisions for the priesthood. Other regulations of the priests are scattered throughout the Pentateuch. Many of these regulations reflect the work of devout priests during the sixth and fifth centuries B.C. who sought in troubled times to redirect the people to the worship of the one true God.

FROM LAW TO LEGALISM

These laws were to serve as a guide for those living as God's people. Through obedience to these laws they would please and praise God. Beginning with the sixth century B.C., there was a development within Judaism which distorted this purpose. Obedience to the laws was no longer seen as a response of praise but as a measurement of righteousness. Trust in men's own saving works of the law replaced the trust in faith in God's promise.

The feeling was that God had told His people just what to do and what not to do. It was the job of the priests and scribes to interpret these rules. By the end of the Old Testament period there were 613 different rules or laws, plus many more interpretations of the law. Even the interpretations had taken on the force of the laws. These rules became the measuring stick of achievement. You were righteous if you obeyed the rules, sinner if you disregarded them.

JESUS AND THE COMMANDMENTS

One Sabbath day Jesus was walking through the countryside with His disciples. They were hungry. So they took some of the ripe heads of grain in their hands, stripped the grain from the stems, rubbed it in their hands, blew the chaff away, and ate the grain.

Some of the Pharisees saw it and accused Jesus and His disciples of *doing what is not lawful on the sabbath* (Mk. 2:24). To pluck heads of grain in a neighbor's field was not considered wrong. But according to the interpretation of the rabbis, prohibition of work on the Sabbath included thirty-nine occupations. Among these were harvesting and threshing. Jesus and the disciples were guilty!

The laws that God had given the Hebrews to regulate the life of the community had become an impossible burden. The many interpretations, the "laws about laws" had become ridiculous.

Take for example the law about Sabbath-keeping. How far could you walk on the Sabbath? Only a certain number of paces from your house was permitted. But some ingenious Pharisees found an old interpretation that a man's house was where he had provisions. So you could get around the travel restrictions if the day before the Sabbath you took food to another house, and from that house to another house, and to another, if these were separated by no more than the prescribed maximum paces permitted.

Jesus objected to this kind of talking around the law. He has scathing words for the scribes and Pharisees in Matthew, chapter 23. *They preach, but do not practice. They bind heavy burdens, hard to bear, and lay them on men's shoulders; but they themselves will not move them with their finger. They do all their deeds to be seen by men. . . . Woe to you, scribes and Pharisees, hypocrites . . . blind guides. . . .*

80

But what was Jesus' attitude toward God's law? In Matthew chapter 5, which is part of Jesus' teaching called the Sermon on the Mount, He explains, *"Think not that I have come to abolish the law and the prophets; I have come not to abolish them but to fulfil them"* (v. 17).

Let's look at some of the examples Jesus gives of how the ancient laws given to the Hebrews were not complete. How does Jesus go beyond the old laws to show the full intent of God's law?

Turn to Matthew 5. List the old law. What does Jesus say? Try to put it into a phrase or sentence.

	Old Law	Jesus' Teaching
vv. 21-26		
vv. 27-30		
vv. 31, 32		
vv. 33-37		
vv. 38-42		
vv. 43-48		

Where does Jesus' concern focus? on the act? the thought behind the act? or both? What does this say about the possibility of being good by keeping the rules? What more is needed?

When asked, "Which is the great commandment?" Jesus replied without hesitation: *"You shall love the Lord your God with all your heart, and with all your soul, and with all your mind. . . . And a second is like it, You shall love your neighbor as yourself. On these two commandments depend all the law and the prophets"* (Mt. 22:34-40).

God's law is the law of love. Not cold prohibition, not a burdensome fence to hold us back, but a positive, active command to *love*!

CHRISTIANS AND THE LAW

About 450 years ago in Europe, the Roman Catholic Church taught a way of salvation that looked something like this. Keep the Ten Commandments and the precepts of the church, such as:

—go to church every Sunday

—give to the support of the church

—keep the marriage laws.

That's all you have to do to avoid sinning. And if you do something over and above these rules, you get some extra credit with God. Now if you end up with a balance in the red (more sins than extra credits) you will have to pay penalties after death in what is known as purgatory. If you end up in the black, over and above what you needed to make it to heaven, this extra is skimmed off and put into the Treasury of Merits. The key to this treasury is in the hands of the Bishop of Rome (the Pope).

Today we reject such a manipulated view of salvation. But we also have our own slot-machine tactics by which we try to assure our salvation and that of our loved ones. Who can tell how many good deeds are done to win some extra "stars," how much money is given to the church out of duty and fear and guilt rather than in glad response to God, and how many prayers are spoken in the belief that the right words will somehow save us?

The catch is that nobody has at death any extra merits that can be parceled around. Every man is called to serve the Lord his God with the whole heart, the whole mind, the whole strength. There is no way you can do a work over and above God's law (if God's law is the law of love).

Paul makes it clear in the letter to the Romans that, *They are justified by his grace as a gift, through the redemption which is in Christ* Jesus (3:24). To the Galatians, Paul wrote, *No man is justified before God by the law; for "He who through faith is righteous shall live"* (Gal. 3:11). Not by our good works, but by God's free gift, by God's *grace* are we saved.

We would like to be told exactly what we should do and cannot do. That seems safer. But it doesn't work that way. To reduce Christianity to a set of rules is to reduce religion to outward actions. Further, it ignores God's love as a free gift. It shifts the focus from God to men. It starts to make people proud. But God alone can forgive sin and remove my guilt. I cannot. The law (a set of rules) may tell me what is demanded of me, but leaves me powerless to fulfill these demands.

Perhaps here lies the very value of the law for the Christian. The law is like heading down a blind alley, and finally discovering there is no way out, without help. In this sense it is our schoolmaster, our teacher, to bring us to Christ (Gal. 3:24). Furthermore, the Christian does not always live at the level of his ideal. Here is a law of behavior to remind us of the higher life we ought to live in response to God's love for us.

But the Christian message is that Christ frees us from enslavement to the law. *For freedom Christ has set us free* (Gal. 5:1). We are free to do anything we please? Paul corrects that idea in Galatians 5:13: *do not use your freedom as an opportunity for the flesh, but through love be servants of one another.* We are now free to love, as we never were before. No longer do we need to be all wrapped up with ourselves, but we can begin to live a life of outgoing concern for others.

The author of First Peter puts it: *Live as free men . . . live as servants of God* (1 Pet. 2:16).

WORDS TO REMEMBER

Commandment. Order given by God to which He expects obedience.

Law. Rules of conduct for a community; the guide for the Hebrew people. Often in Christian usage, the Old Testament commandments.

Legalism. When religion focuses on rules, and misses the spirit or intent of God's commands.

Torah. Hebrew word for law. First five books of the Old Testament.

MORE ABOUT CHRISTIANS, LAW AND FREEDOM

1. Read a Bible dictionary article on the Pharisees and scribes.

What was their attitude toward the law? What examples of Pharisaism do you see among Christians today?

2. Why is legalistic religion inadequate? Mennonites are sometimes charged with being legalistic. Why do you think the charge is made? In what ways may it be true or not true?

3. Can we live without any rules of conduct? Why or why not?

4. Regarding God's law, some contend there are certain fixed eternal principles laid down once for all. Others contend that each human situation calls for making of decisions in light of the circumstances at the time. For example, during World War II a Dutch pastor gave shelter to several Jews. When the Nazi troops came to the house to inquire about any Jews being hidden there, the pastor denied it. In this situation he felt the truth would have meant the murder of his friends. What value and what problems do you see in this kind of decision making?

5. What does Christian freedom mean to a high school student in relation to his home, school, church, and community?

19. Arthur Gilbert, *Your Neighbor Worships* (New York: Anti-Defamation League of B'nai B'rith), pp. 14-18.

Chapter 12

Jesus -- Human and Divine

Michael Munkacsy's famous painting, *Christ Before Pilate* was on exhibit in Hamilton, Ontario. A sailor from one of the lake boats pushed his way to the door of the exhibit hall. "Is Christ here? How much to see Christ?" he growled to the woman in attendance.

Grumbling, he paid the admission, and swaggered into the room. He sat down in the front of the great picture, studying it for a few minutes. Off came his hat. Picking up the descriptive folder he had dropped on the floor when he sat down, he began to read and to study the picture. Now and then he dropped his face into his hands. An hour later he left the hall with tears in his eyes.

I came here to see Christ.

"Madam," he said, "I came here to see Christ because my mother asked me to. I only came to please her. I am a rough man sailing on the lakes. I never believed in any such thing, but a man who could paint a picture like that must have believed in it. And there is something in it that makes me believe in it, too."[20]

What is this strange power that confronts us in Jesus Christ? Who is this Man that changes men? Who is this Christ whom Christians claim as Lord of life?

Most of us have studied about Jesus all our lives. But who is He? What did He do? What is He like? What makes Him unique? What is He to us?

In this session we will look at the sources for our knowledge of Jesus, an outline of major events in His life, and the claim that Jesus is the Son of God. In the sessions that follow, we will try to discover the meaning of His death on the cross and the resurrection.

OUR SOURCES OF INFORMATION ABOUT JESUS

Had Jesus been born in the latter half of the twentieth century, we could get a complete record of Him. Imagine the flashbulbs popped to record every detail of His face, the films recording His actions, the miles of tape recording His voice, the stacks of printed copies of His talks! Think of the many on-the-spot interviews with those touched by His life. And somewhere there would be a duly registered birth certificate.

But in those days, nearly two thousand years ago, people were not as historically-minded. Nor did they have the fancy equipment to record a life the way we can. This makes it all the more exciting to realize how full a picture of Jesus of Nazareth we actually do have.

It is true that outside the New Testament we find scant reference to Jesus in the writings available to us from the first century. There is reference to Jesus by Tacitus, the Roman historian, and in the *Talmud,* a Jewish encyclopedia. Josephus, a Jewish historian living A.D. 37-100, alludes to Jesus in his *Antiquities of the Jews*. He also gives helpful background to our understanding of the Jewish groups in Jesus' day, the Sadducees, Pharisees, Scribes, and Essenes.

The records of the Qumran community, which existed during the time Jesus lived, do not refer to Jesus. But they help to substantiate our understanding of the fanatic sects of Judaism of Jesus' day. There are references to Jesus in the "Apocryphal Gospels" written later in the first century, but these are fanciful accounts.

And so we look at the records we have in the church's book, the New Testament. Here we have the Gospels according to Matthew, Mark, Luke, and John. In addition we learn about Jesus from the sermons of Peter and Paul in the Book of Acts, and in the Letters to the churches.

The Gospels are not complete biographies. Each presents a portrait of Jesus, through the eyes of faith. Each is an eyewitness account, and written with a special purpose.

Mark, the earliest account we have, was written at least twenty to twenty-five years after Jesus' death. The Gospel writers had access to some written sources, as well as the sayings and deeds of Jesus as remembered by the persons who had been with Him. Most of Mark's account is included in the Gospels written by Matthew and Luke, suggesting that these men had access to Mark's writing.

Below is a brief summary of characteristics of the four Gospels. For more detail you may wish to read an introduction to the New Testament or a Bible dictionary article on each of the Gospels.

Gospel	Date Written	Characteristics or Purpose	Portrait of Jesus
Mark	50-65	Brief, vivid fast-moving action. May have been written at Rome for Roman Christians.	Presents Jesus as the strong man of action, Jesus as Son of man and Son of God.
Matthew	65-70	Written for people of Jewish background to witness that Jesus was the Messiah of the Old Testament promises and that His mission was to bring the kingdom of God to men. Perhaps used as a book for teaching catechumens.	Presents Jesus as the fulfillment and great teacher of the Law.

Luke	64-70	Written primarily for people of Gentile background by a Greek. Includes especially the stories of Jesus' concern for all kinds of people.	Presents Jesus as the divine Savior, who came to befriend also the poor, the outcast, women, foreigners—all men.
John	69-90	". . . written that you may believe that Jesus is the Christ, the Son of God, and that believing you may have life in his name" (Jn. 20:30, 31). Less concern with order of events than with what these things mean.	Presents Jesus as the Divine Word of God made flesh, the One who is the light and life of the world.

THE LIFE OF JESUS IN OUTLINE

Using mainly Mark's order of events, let us look at the major periods and key events in Jesus' life:

1. The Period of Preparation   1:1-13

    Ministry of John the Baptist   1:1-8

    (For the birth stories we need to turn to Matthew 1:18—2:23 and Luke 1 and 2.)

    Baptism, commitment to the task and testing the mission 1:9-13

2. Galilean Ministry   1:14—9:50

    Calling disciples   1:14-20

    Deeds of mercy, the signs and miracles   1:21-45

    Teachings   4:1-20   (Here Matthew 5—7, the Sermon on the Mount, is a good sample.)

    Opposition   2:23—3:6

    Sending out the disciples   6:7-13

3. Caesarea Philippi   8:27—9:50

    Peter's confession, "You are the Christ."   8:27—9:1

    The transfiguration   9:2-29

4. The Passion Week

    Journey toward Jerusalem   10:1-52

    Entry of city, cleansing the temple, teachings   11:1—14:11

    The Last Supper   14:12-25

Life of Christ.

Garden, arrest, trial   14:26—15:20
Crucifixion and burial   15:21-47
5. The Resurrection and Great Commission   16:1-20 and
Matthew 28

ONE INTERPRETATION OF THE MAN, JESUS

From a purely human viewpoint, the story of Jesus could be written like this:

"Here is a man who was born in an obscure village, the child of a peasant woman. He grew up in another obscure village. He worked in a carpenter shop until He was thirty, and then for three years He was an itinerant preacher. He never wrote a book. He never held an office.

"He never owned a home. He never set foot inside a big city. He never traveled two hundred miles from the place where He was born. He had no credentials but himself.

"He had nothing to do with this world except the naked power of His divine manhood. While still a young man, the tide of popular opinion turned against Him. His friends ran away. One of them betrayed Him. He was turned over to His enemies. He went through the mockery of a trial. He was nailed upon a cross between two thieves.

"His executioners gambled for the only piece of property He had on earth while He was dying . . . His coat. When He was dead, He was taken down and laid in a borrowed grave through the pity of a friend."[21]

ANOTHER INTERPRETATION—JESUS, SON OF GOD

There is more of course. Through the eyes of faith we begin to see plan and purpose in the life of Jesus.

Birth

The lowly, miraculous birth of this baby to a peasant virgin girl, the family life at Nazareth, a happy childhood in a little country village, the tasks of the carpenter's shop, and the growing consciousness of God are an important part of Jesus' early life.

Mission

Then came the call to His mission at about age thirty. John the Baptist, the revival preacher of the Jordan, played an important part as Jesus went to him for baptism. In this act, Jesus committed himself to God's mission and received the power of the Spirit of God for His task. Following baptism there was a period of testing that mission. In the temptations Jesus faced we see the reality of His humanity.

Then the Gospels tell us that Jesus returned to Galilee *preaching the gospel of God* (Mk. 1:14). The nature of Jesus' work was that of a traveling preacher and teacher. Sometimes He was in a synagogue taking part in the service. Or He might be in a home with the people crowding about the door to hear Him. And again, He might be walking alone by the sea.

He was a person deeply charged with a sense of mission, and He presented His message with boldness. Crowds soon flocked around Him as the common people heard Him gladly. He was concerned about persons and their needs. He healed the sick, befriended outcasts, and brought men into right relation with God.

Opposition

But then came opposition from the religious authorities of the day as Jesus challenged the accepted standards of goodness and criticized hypocrisy in religion. He urged men to count the cost before they decided to follow Him. The authorities tried to silence Him. His own countrymen drove Him out of their cities. Even His family wondered if He was mad.

Toward Jerusalem

But Jesus did not veer from His course. The Gospels report that after a time of preaching Jesus withdrew to the north with His disciples to a place called Caesarea Philippi. Here in a climactic conversation with His disciples, they expressed belief in Him as the long-expected Messiah of the Jews. It was here that He set His face toward Jerusalem to participate in the annual spring festival of the Jewish religion, the Feast of Passover.

91

Death

In Jerusalem His dramatic act of forcing profiteers out of the temple further antagonized the Jewish officials. Here the Jewish religious leaders succeeded in bringing Him to trial and death. Through the betrayal of one of His own disciples, false charges, and an improper trial He was brought to tragic death—the humiliating and painful death of hanging on a cross.

RESURRECTION

The story of a life, a hope, a movement ordinarily would end here. But this one does not. Rather than being the end of the story, it is the beginning. There was an initial sense of defeat after His death. The disciples feared that they too might be caught, tried, and put to death. But then the risen Christ appeared to them. Surprised, doubting, not knowing how to explain this new phenomenon at first, they gathered around Him once again and drew themselves together to gain courage. Their eyes were opened to a new sense of His leadership and power among them that they had not known before. His living reality has been shared by Christians down through the centuries.

WHAT WAS JESUS LIKE?

1. He was *a real human being*. There is no doubt about the fact that Jesus of Nazareth lived as a real person in history. He worked, played, laughed, cried, was tempted, was discouraged, and suffered pain. His humanity reminds us that God drew close to our flesh and blood. In Christ's earthly life He experienced our humanity firsthand.

2. He was *a masculine person*. Sometimes the pictures of Jesus we have seen have left us with the impression of an effeminate, meek creature. As eldest son of a family of eight, His work at the carpenter's bench would have built muscles and callouses. Rough-and-ready fishermen like Peter, James, and John were attracted enough to leave their nets and follow Him. He was strong and manly, yet gentle and tender.

3. He was *brave*. He opposed phony religion. He set His face

steadfastly toward Jerusalem even when He knew it would likely cost His life.

4. He *loved all kinds of people.* He wanted the best for people. Whether they were rich, poor, educated, common, old, young, friends or enemies, He loved them.

5. He was *very close to God.* That closeness to God began early. Matthew 1:18-25 and Luke 1:26-38 remind us that God was His Father. Even at the age of twelve Jesus recognized His special relationship to God (Lk. 2:49). People came to speak of Him as "Emmanuel," "God with us," "the Son of God."[22]

HIS CLAIM TO UNIQUENESS

Unique means more than simply unusual. It means "one-of-a-kind." What makes Jesus unique?

It is not entirely His fame as a teacher. There have been other great teachers. Nor can it be His strong personality or His meekness. But we find it in the claim that He is fully God—God in the form of man. When Jesus speaks of himself as "Son of man" (Mk. 14:61, 62; 2:10), He is identifying himself with the hope of the promised Messiah.

In John 10:30-33 Jesus says, "I and the Father are one." Those who heard the claim accused Him of claiming to be God, and tried to stone Him. The impact of what He was saying was clear to them. In fact, He was crucified because the Jewish people accused Him of blasphemy.

Either He was God's Son in whom God dwelt on earth, or He was an impostor—for He did not deny the charges against Him. Christians believe that He is truly the Son of God.

WORDS TO REMEMBER

Gospel. Literally means "good news." The four accounts of Jesus' life written by Matthew, Mark, Luke, and John.

Incarnation. Becoming flesh or human; the coming of God in the person of Jesus.

Messiah. A word used frequently in the Old Testament meaning one called or anointed by God. The Greek word for Messiah is *Christos,* which we translate "Christ."

Lord. One who holds power over other beings. The New Testament takes the word *Lord* as used for God and applies it to Jesus.

TO GAIN A NEW UNDERSTANDING OF JESUS

1. Read through the Gospel of Mark at one sitting. Try to catch the movement, the action of this Person as He encounters men, and their response to Him.

What effect did Jesus have on the people who knew Him best?

What kind of people did He choose to be close to Him?

Were there any people who had a chance to follow Him and decided not to?

Were there any secret disciples?

Were there any rules or requirements for being a follower?

Did His disciples ever let Him down?

2. Using a Bible dictionary try to find out as much as you can about the background of His times.

What was the land like?

What were the Jewish groups like?

Pharisees

Sadducees

Scribes

Zealots

Essenes

What was the political situation? What was Jesus' attitude toward the Romans?

3. What about Jesus attracts, impresses, or repels people? How do you feel about Jesus?

20. Cynthia Pearl Maus, *Christ and the Fine Arts* (New York: Harper and Brothers, 1938), p. 363.

21. Gerald Kennedy, *A Reader's Notebook* (New York: Harper and Brothers, 1953), p. 147.

22. Nevin C. Harner, *I Believe* (Philadelphia: United Church, 1950), pp. 15-20.

Chapter 13

The Meaning of the Cross

And you, who were dead in trespasses. . . , God made alive together with him, having forgiven us all our trespasses, having canceled the bond which stood against us with its legal demands; this he set aside, nailing it to the cross. He disarmed the principalities and powers and made a public example of them, triumphing over them in him. Colossians 2:13-15

A hangman's noose dangling over the communion table? An electric chair against the front wall of the sanctuary? "Why not?" suggested a man concerned that most of us never see the symbol there now—the cross.

Crosses—you've seen them. On church spires, carved in pulpits, imprinted on hymnbook covers, hanging on a chain around someone's neck, decorating tombstones. Crosses—of rugged wood, shining metal, polished stones, and glaring neon. Crosses—so much a part of our landscape, we hardly notice them.

It was different nineteen hundred years ago. A cross standing on a hillside spoke of horrible pain and slow, tortuous death. Used by the Romans, the cross was reserved for the punishment and execution of the worst criminal offenders.

And now we find it decorating everything in the church. Why? Why has the cross become the central symbol of the Christian church?

CENTRALITY OF THE CROSS IN THE NEW TESTAMENT

In the earliest writings we have, Paul's letters, the death and resurrection of Jesus Christ take central place. *For I delivered unto you first of all that which I also received, how that Christ died for our sins* (1 Cor. 15:3 KJV). For Paul, the gospel concerned *Jesus Christ and him crucified* (1 Cor. 2:2).

The early preaching recorded in the Book of Acts has the same emphasis. Peter at Pentecost declares: *This Jesus . . . you crucified and killed by the hands of lawless men* (Acts 2:23).

And in the Gospels, where we have the fullest description of Jesus' healing and teaching ministry, the focus also is upon the death and resurrection of Jesus Christ. The amount of space devoted to the events of the last week in Jesus' life on earth and the resurrection account includes:

Gospel	Section	Percentage of total book
Matthew	21:1—28:20	28%
Mark	11:1—16:8	37%
Luke	19:28—24:53	23%
John	12:12—21:25	41%

THE EVENT

"You are the Christ, the Son of the living God," Peter had declared. "You are Christ—the one anointed by God!" Jesus accepted this confession of faith from His disciples. From Caesarea Philippi He set his face toward Jerusalem (Mk. 8:31). Many were moving toward Jerusalem to participate in the annual Feast of Passover.

The swift-moving events of that last week include:

a triumphal entry into the city amid crowds who hailed Him King,

daily teaching to the crowds that gathered around Him,

Jesus' dramatic act of forcing the profiteers out of the temple, which was an open clash with the authorities.

Then came that Last Supper with His disciples,

and prayer in Gethsemane:

"Father, if thou art willing, remove this cup from me;

nevertheless not my will, but thine, be done" (Lk. 22:42).

The betrayal by one of his own group, Judas,

Death of Jesus.

BARABBAS
NAIL HIM
TO THE CROSS!
KILL HIM!

arrest,
trial before the Jewish court, the Sanhedrin,
and Pilate,
and Herod,
and Pilate again.
Finally, the sentence of death at the hands of the angry mob,
the mocking soldiers,
and then that long walk out of the city
to the place called Golgotha, the Skull.

In your Bible, read one of the four accounts of that Good Friday:

Matthew 27:32-60
Mark   15:21-47
Luke   23:26-56
John   19:17-42

As you read, look for and record the following:

1. Who witnessed the death of Jesus? What effect did Jesus' death have upon the various people mentioned?

2. What is striking to you about the way Jesus died, about the person He was in death?

WHAT DOES IT MEAN?

Why should the death of Jesus be so crucial to the Christian faith? Others have died in the vigor of life, in the prime of their work. Other innocent men have been unjustly put to death. What special meaning is there in Jesus' death?

Here are three of the most common words and ideas the Bible uses to describe this event:

1. *Justification.* Here is a word picture from the practice of law. The word represents God's justice. Paul writes to the Galatians, "that no man is justified by the law in the sight of God, it is evident: for, The just shall live by faith" (3:11 KJV). God has declared us just, righteous, acceptable.

God is a God of holiness and justice. He cannot tolerate sin. Sin must be taken seriously, and dealing with it costs. Sin requires punishment. The idea expressed here is that Jesus has "taken the rap" for us. We are free men, for our pardon has been purchased by Jesus Christ.

"Justification is that immediate setting right with God which God himself accomplishes by His grace when man has faith" (N. H. Smith). Justification means that God through Jesus declared us acceptable, "just-as-if" we had not sinned.

2. *Atonement.* This word represents God's love. The idea comes from the Old Testament practice of sacrifice. A lamb, a dove, some grain was brought to the altar and sacrificed as a substitute, as a covering for human sin. Jesus Christ has become the "sacrifice" for us. "We also joy in God through our Lord Jesus Christ, by whom we have now received the atonement" (Rom. 5:11 KJV). Jesus came to be called "the Lamb of God" (Jn. 1:29). Check also Romans 3:25 and Hebrews 9 and 10.

Atonement means literally "at-one-ment," to be made one with God. This is the meaning also of the word *reconcile* used by Paul in Romans 5:10 and 2 Corinthians 5:19.

Atonement is a covering of our sins whereby they are treated as nonexistent and the sinner as if he had not committed them. No, our sins are not condoned and forgotten. We must confess them and find forgiveness. But we can be reconciled to God through Christ. We can be delivered from a condition of estrangement, and restored to fellowship with God. The healing process has been initiated by God.

3. *Redeem* or *Ransom.* These words represent God's gift. The words come from the practice of buying back something which originally belonged to the purchaser. A man redeems a note in the bank when he pays off his debt. Or the early Christians would have seen in this word the picture of a slave set free when his master was paid a stipulated sum.

Jesus Christ came *"not to be served but to serve, and to give his life as a ransom for many"* (Mk. 10:45). He paid the price so that we could be God's children.

The Japanese Christian, Kagawa, once was asked which theory

describing the value for us in Jesus' death he favored. Kagawa replied:

"I think just as Paul did. Paul felt that there was something wrong with man, and Christ could make him right. When Paul tried to say what was wrong with men, he used parables. Now it was a debtor whose debts must be paid; again a condemned criminal to be relieved; a sick man to be healed; a dead man to be raised; a slave to be emancipated; or a wandering child to be brought home. But," added Kagawa, his face aglow, "Paul didn't care which parable you used, or if you used some other. All he cared about was that man was somehow wrong, and Christ could set him right."[23]

The emphasis in all of these words and ideas is that God has acted in holy love. God has taken the first step in our salvation. It is our responsibility to recognize and accept God's forgiveness.

WE ARE IMPORTANT TO GOD

God has a heart of love that reaches out to us continually. Jesus tells three stories about the lost (Luke 15), a lost sheep, a lost coin, and a lost son. He emphasizes not so much that which was lost, but the seeking for the lost. The shepherd went out looking for the one lamb that had wandered off by itself. The woman who lost the coin sought diligently. The father, though he did not track down his rebellious son, also sought patiently and hopefully.

Jesus is saying here that God is seeking. God is calling, searching, waiting hopefully, because we are precious to Him. As long as we are lost, out of a right relation with Him, His heart will not rest. And that is what Jesus' death on the cross is saying to us. *The Son of God who loved me and gave himself for me* (Gal. 2:20).

God doesn't stand off on the side like an umpire. But God in Christ came down into human life. He got himself involved with us. And so reconciliation may take place, not from somewhere off on the side, but from within, from the life we know.

100

THE PAIN AND JOY OF FORGIVENESS

The play, *A Man of God,* by the French writer, Gabriel Marcel, tells the story of Claude and Edmee Lemoyne. Early in their married life, Edmee had betrayed her husband. Claude knew of the affair when it happened. Following months of inner agony, his decision had been to offer his wife his complete forgiveness.

In retrospect he says, "Yes, I forgave her. And I shall never forget what that did for me, the inner peace it brought, the sense of a Power working with me."

Claude had imagined through the years that both his and God's forgiveness had been accepted by Edmee, and that the matter was a closed book. When it suddenly is reopened by the appearance of the other man, he discovers that Edmee has been completely unable to accept his forgiveness. Her whole life has been colored by the fact that, although forgiven, she could not accept forgiveness.

Claude again declares his forgiveness. What else can he do? But when he reminds his wife that he has forgiven her, he is astonished when she replies: "I'm sick of your tolerance. I'm sick of your broadmindedness. It nauseates me. What do you expect me to do with all this generosity that cost you nothing?"

"Nothing, when I forgave you?" he asks.[24]

Does our failure to recognize the cost of forgiveness prevent us from accepting God's forgiving love demonstrated by Christ's self-giving death?

One Sunday, when H. H. Farmer was preaching on the love of God, an old Polish Jew who had been converted to the Christian faith came to him after the service. "You have no right to speak about the love of God," he said, "until you have seen, as I have seen, the blood of your dearest friends running in the gutters on a gray winter morning."

Then he explained. It was on that gray morning, in those blood-stained streets, that the Christian gospel began to lay hold on him. For it bade him see God—the love of God—just where he was.

"As I looked at that man upon the cross, as I heard him pray,

'Father, forgive them, for they know not what they do,' as I heard him cry in his anguish, 'My God, My God, why hast thou forsaken me?' I knew that I was at a point of final crisis and decision in my life; I knew that I must make up my mind once and for all, and either take my stand beside him and share in his undefeated faith in God . . . or else fall finally into a bottomless pit of bitterness, hatred, and despair."[25]

WORDS TO REMEMBER

Atonement. At-one-ment; reconciliation between men and God through Christ.

Justification. God's act in Christ, declaring sinful man just; just-as-if he had not sinned.

Redemption. (Redeem, Ransom) Rescued or delivered from slavery by payment of a price, as Christ gave His life to free us from bondage to sin.

Sacrifice. An offering to God; giving oneself for some other person, as Christ's giving His life to save man.

Forgiveness. To cover up, carry away, let go; the healing of a broken relationship; God's free gift to us.

WHAT DO THE CROSS AND GOD'S GIFT OF SALVATION MEAN TO YOU?

1. If salvation is the free gift of God, why do people find it so hard to believe and accept?

2. Next time you see the cross, whether at the front of the church, or elsewhere, stop for a moment to think about it. Think of the cross as being about fifteen feet high, hewn out of rough beams, standing on a windswept hill. Think of a man hanging on it—straining in that half-conscious state of thirst and exhaustion and unbearable pain. Think of Jesus' sad, yet kind face. Think of the love God has for you.

3. God's plan and act for our redemption is the very heart of the gospel. Gospel means "good news." In what way is this good news? In what way is this good news to you?

OUR PRAYER

Christ, we do all adore Thee
And we do praise Thee forever.
For on the holy cross hast Thou
    the world from sin redeemed.
Christ, we do all adore Thee!

      —Dubois, *The Seven Last Words.*

23. J. Carter Swaim, "Atone-ment," *International Journal of Religious Education,* 37:5 (January 1961), p. 3.

24. Gabriel Marcel, *A Man of God, Ariadne, the Funeral Pyre* (Secker and Warburg, Ltd., 1952), pp. 47, 59.

25. Robert Clyde Johnson, *The Meaning of Christ* (Philadelphia: Westminster Press, 1958), pp. 46, 47.

Chapter 14

Jesus -- the Living Lord

For I delivered to you as of first importance what I also received, that Christ died for our sins in accordance with the scriptures, that he was buried, that he was raised on the third day in accordance with the scriptures, and that he appeared . . . he appeared also to me. 1 Corinthians 15:3-8

Every book in the New Testament declares or assumes that Jesus rose from the dead. This event took place on "the third day," on Sunday morning, after Jesus was crucified on Friday afternoon.

QUESTIONS ABOUT THE RESURRECTION

There are those who can accept the historical reliability of the New Testament record concerning Jesus' life until they come to the event of His resurrection. Here they balk. This, they feel, just cannot be true. They look for other explanations like the following:

1. Jesus took a drug. He was not really dead, but was assumed to be dead.
2. "Heroes do not die." The disciples were stubbornly sure that Jesus would not die, and therefore since they expected to see Him risen, they projected His image into the appearances recorded in the Gospels.
3. Jesus communicated with the disciples after His death in a kind of telepathy rather than in the appearance of a visibly material body.

But resurrection? They conclude that the church must have created this story. But in fact it is the other way around. The truth of the resurrection created the church.

Theologian Emil Brunner states it this way, "That the message of the early church is the witness to the resurrection of Jesus, that it was the appearances of the risen Lord which brought the shattered and scattered disciples together again after the catastrophe of Good Friday, and formed the real foundation of the Christian church—stands upon such firm ground, that even the unbelieving historian cannot get away from it."[26]

WITNESS TO THE RESURRECTION

1. Read 1 Corinthians 15:1-8. Make a list of the appearances of the risen Christ Paul mentions here.

2. What is the recurring theme in Peter's sermons recorded in Acts? Check Acts 2:24, 32; 3:15; 4:10; 5:30.

3. Study each of the Gospel accounts and try to answer these questions: Who saw Jesus? What was He like? What did He say? How did the person or persons respond?

Passage   Who?   Jesus appearance   Jesus' words   The response

1. Mark 16:1-8
2. Matthew 28:1-10
3. Matthew 28:16-20
4. Luke 24:1-11
5. Luke 24:13-25
6. Luke 24:36-53
7. John 20:1-18
8. John 20:19-23
9. John 20:24-29
10. John 21:1-25

Note: Other ancient texts and versions include a longer ending to Mark's Gospel. This can be found in a footnote at the end of Mark in the Revised Standard Version, or in the King James Version.

    Mark 16:9-11
    Mark 16:12, 13
    Mark 16:14-20

As you look over these resurrection appearances listed in the Gospels, what do you observe? For example: Who and what kind

Truly this man was the Son of God!

of people saw Jesus? Did any who were not followers recognize Him? What do we learn as to what the resurrection body of Jesus was like? Write down as many observations as you can.

THE EVIDENCE

Merrill C. Tenney examines in detail the available evidence in his book, *The Reality of the Resurrection.*[27]

He points out that a striking feature of the Gospel accounts is the emphasis on the certainty of Jesus' death. That Jesus died and was not just drugged or in a coma is verified by:

The comment of the centurion (Mk. 15:39).

The physical results of the spear thrust into Jesus' side (Jn. 19:34).

The official pronouncement of the government (Mk. 15:43, 44).

The obvious intention of the women who came to the tomb.

The burial by His aristocratic friends, Joseph of Arimathea and Nicodemus.

Tenney then classifies and investigates the different kinds of evidence for the resurrection:

1. The material evidence
    the displaced stone
    the empty tomb
    the graveclothes
2. The physical appearances of Jesus
3. The historical results
    the transformation of the disciples
    the descent of the Holy Spirit
    the church

We have already studied the appearances of Jesus. You may want to do some more detective work on the stone, the tomb, and the graveclothes. But now let's examine the results of the resurrection, particularly the church.

THE CHURCH, AS EVIDENCE OF THE RESURRECTION

Think back to that dark Good Friday. The Gospels tell us that when Jesus was taken by the soldiers in the Garden of Gethsemane the disciples "forsook him and fled" (Mt. 26:56; Mk. 14:50). Peter followed at a distance. But when attention is turned toward him, he denied knowledge of Jesus, "I don't know the man!"

Some of the disciples were present at the crucifixion, but the circle was broken. They were scattered. Their Master was gone. Their hopes were dashed. Disillusioned and afraid, they met on that first day of the week. John says, "The doors being shut . . . for fear of the Jews" (Jn. 20:19).

But it was not all over. The day when men were surest that they were rid of Jesus was the day before His resurrection. The word that changed these fearful, disillusioned, scattered disciples into a band of fearless, convinced missionaries was the word, "He is risen!" He met them again; Christ was alive. He returned from death to be with them.

No, it was not the same as before. The sobering experiences of the past days and Jesus' words at that Last Supper, "I go away . . ." were not yet forgotten. But Jesus Christ was alive and present. He talked with them. He ate with them, though His risen body was different from our ordinary bodies.

Then came that day when they would see Jesus no longer. The Book of Acts tells the story of the ascension. Jesus spoke to His followers a final time, reminding them to be His witnesses, and reassuring them that power would be given them (Acts 1:8). Then Jesus disappeared from their sight.

Ten days later, now fifty days after the crucifixion,[28] the disciples were again together in a room in Jerusalem. An unmistakable power and presence filled the room and the persons present.

Peter's sermon comes to a climax with the declaration, *"This Jesus God raised up, and of that we all are witnesses. Being therefore exalted at the right hand of God, and having received from the Father the promise of the Holy Spirit, he has poured out this which you see and hear. . . . Let all . . . know assuredly that God has made him both Lord and Christ, this Jesus whom you crucified"* (Acts 2:32-36).

From that encounter with the living Spirit of Jesus Christ the disciples went out into the world. The disciples became apostles —the ones sent out to witness to God's supreme act of redemption. When Peter and John dared to stand up and preach to the high priest about Jesus, they were warned not to speak in the name of Jesus anymore. But they answered, "We cannot but speak of what we have seen and heard" (Acts 4:20).

And speak they did! Within twenty years there were groups of Christians scattered throughout the cities of the Roman Empire. The momentum of this new movement threatened not only the Jewish religion, but the Roman Empire as well. "The men who have turned the world upside down have come here! They preach that there is another king besides Caesar, another king named Jesus!"

Even when finally the full force of the Roman Empire was pitted against Christians, their property confiscated, the believers jailed or fined, beheaded, thrown to the wild beasts in the arena— their belief in a living Lord could not be shaken. Polycarp, Bishop of Smyrna during the first half of the second century, had been one of those who met and talked with people who had actually known Jesus. When he was arrested and brought before a howling stadium mob to face a martyr's death, he was given one more chance to recant, "Swear by the fortune of Caesar, and I set you free; curse Christ!"

But Polycarp calmly replied: "Eighty and six years have I served Him, and He did me no wrong. How can I blaspheme Him, my Lord and My King?"

THE RESURRECTION—AND US

We cannot explain the resurrection. This is miracle. And the New Testament writers are not concerned about explaining it. Their main concern is to proclaim the resurrection of Jesus and the power of Jesus' living presence.

We dare not ignore the New Testament's message about the resurrection and the ascension, even though we may not understand it. For it says that the work of Jesus did not end on the cross on Good Friday, or even at the empty tomb at Easter. His ministry continues even now. What may this mean for us?

1. *God reigns.* The fact that Jesus triumphed over death was proof of His lordship. He was not defeated, but victorious even over the worst that men could do to Him. Paul says: *Christ died and lived again, that he might be Lord both of the dead and of the living* (Rom. 14:9). In this, Christians have placed their hope.

Martin Niemoeller, the great German pastor who spent eight years from 1937-1945 in a Nazi concentration camp, tells about one Easter while in prison. On the Thursday of Easter week, 1941, Niemoeller was being escorted along the main road of Camp Sachsenhausen to meet a visitor.

Along the edge of the road he noticed a word scratched into

the gravel, apparently by one of the prisoners whose job it was to keep the road in repair.

It was a Latin word—*VIVIT—HE LIVES!* The Easter message deeply engraved in the soil of Sachsenhausen—soil soaked with the blood of the dead! Who can say what comfort it brought to the prisoners who saw it. And to how many it gave hope to live on.

2. *Jesus' power over all, yet personal concern.* The ascension or "exaltation" was an important theme of the early church. Jesus being exalted to the right hand of God was a way of speaking about His living and continued work (Eph. 1:19, 20). The seat on the right hand of an oriental king was always reserved for his prime minister, who shared his authority and dignity. Jesus shares God's rule.

But the ongoing work of Christ includes standing with us. Paul writes of *Christ Jesus, who died, yes, who was raised from the de d, who is at the right hand of God, who indeed intercedes for us* (Rom. 8:34). John writes, *". . . should anyone commit a sin, we have one to plead our cause with the Father, Jesus Christ"* (1 John 2:1 NEB). And so we dare to pray "in the name of Jesus" or in desperation blurt out, "God, I need help!"

3. *New life.* The resurrection sets the pattern for a new life. Paul's writings glow with this new spirit.

God . . . made us alive together with Christ . . . (Eph. 2:5).

If then you have been raised with Christ, seek the things that are above . . . (Col. 3:1).

. . . the upward call of God in Christ Jesus (Phil. 3:14).

It is no longer I who live, but Christ who lives in me; and the life I now live in the flesh I live by faith in the Son of God, who loved me and gave himself for me (Gal. 2:20).

An eagle that is born to soar in the open sky cannot be content in the confinement of a cage. His ambition and his strength are matched with the clouds and the mountain heights. A person who has sensed God's love in Christ, and has become aware of the power of Christ's presence, can no longer be satisfied in pleasing himself.

The astounding claim is that Jesus Christ is alive today, ready and powerful to enter the life of anyone who invites Him to come in.

WORDS TO REMEMBER

Resurrection. Becoming alive again, as Jesus' rising from the dead.

Ascension. Fortieth day after Jesus' resurrection when His disciples saw Him for the last time.

Right hand of God. Position of honor and power in relation to God.

THE DIFFERENCE EASTER MAKES

1. Easter is the church's special yearly celebration of the resurrection. Easter is preceded by a forty-six day period of preparation called Lent. Likewise, the Easter season includes a forty-day period, from Easter to Ascension Day. Of what value can the Lenten and Easter season be in helping you experience Christ's presence?

2. The Christian practice of having worship on Sunday rather than on the Sabbath as the Jews did, stems from the fact that the early Christians met on the "first day of the week" to celebrate Jesus' resurrection. This Sunday as you worship, think about the exciting truth that you are celebrating the resurrection! What difference will this make in your worship? in your living?

3. "We cannot build cathedrals in the shape of an empty tomb. We cannot adequately paint a picture of the resurrection. We cannot place a symbol of the resurrection around our necks or on our hymnals. We must *be* living symbols of that resurrection."[29]

26. Emil Brunner, *The Christian Doctrine of Creation and Redemption,* trans. Olive Wyon (Philadelphia: Westminster Press, 1952), p. 366.

27. Merrill C. Tenney, *The Reality of the Resurrection* (New York: Harper and Row, 1963), pp. 105ff.

28. The date is arrived at by reference to the Jewish festivals of Passover (Luke 22:1) and Pentecost (Acts 2:1).

29. Elaine Sommers Rich, Faith and Life Press Church Bulletin #4662.

Chapter 15

How Do I Become a Christian?

But to all who received him, who believed in his name, he gave
power to become children of God. . . .   John 1:12

"I believe in God and try to do what He wants me to, but like to do what I want to better."

"Many times I have given myself up to God, but it seems that I never get the feeling I am really saved. I try to be kind and thoughtful, but sometimes lose control of my temper. I feel embarrassed and afraid to talk about it with someone."

"I always thought I was a Christian since I grew up in a Christian home. Now as I grow older and begin studying more about it, I know it is not that way. You have to take Him in through your own way, and let Him become your personal Savior."

"I pray that I may become a Christian, but I don't feel any different."

"Am I supposed to know the day I became a Christian? Is there always a definite time when you become a Christian, or can it happen over a period of weeks or months?"

Here are the expressions of young teens as they share their struggles in committing themselves to Christ and understanding their faith. Have you had some of the same feelings? What are your questions about becoming a Christian?

Let's begin with a basic one . . .

WHO IS A CHRISTIAN?

What would you say? One who keeps the Golden Rule? One who tithes? One who doesn't swear, smoke, or drink? In chapter 11, when we talked about the commandments, we discarded that idea.

It isn't what we *don't do,* nor what we *do,* that makes us Christians. Nor is a Christian simply one who has grown up in a home where people call themselves Christians or go to church. Who is a Christian?

A Christian is one who responds to the call of Christ. A Christian is a person who trusts Him when He says, "I have given you the pledge of salvation, follow me." The Christian finds in God's love through Christ the power that rescues from the penalty and consequences of sin and sets him free to begin to respond in joyful service with his whole life.

How does this come about in our lives? Read the profiles of the two young Christians, Louie and Rod. What does becoming a Christian mean to them? In what ways is the experience of each in becoming a Christian different from that of the other? How are these like or unlike your experience in learning to know and accept Christ as your Savior and Lord?

Louie

Louie calls a two-room apartment on 45th Street home. But you won't find him there. Too crowded, with three younger brothers and two sisters and his mother. . . . Besides, Louie has a job. He referees basketball games for the younger kids down at the community center. Louie's proud of that job. But let's hear him tell it:

"Me? I'm Louie. The Kid—they used to call me. 'Toughest kid on the block!' The little kid's 'ud run when they seen me comin'. But I'll tell you who was scared. Me. Runnin' scared, I tell you. Even when I joined the Panthers, and got to be Big Panther. Scared, I tell you.

"But a funny thing happened. Man, you won't believe it. That night we rolled the old man in the park for a coupla bucks . . . an' got picked up . . . there was this guy Hedley. He stuck out his neck for us. Told the judge not to send us up, but that he believed in us. 'Give me a chance with the fellows,' he told the judge.

"I couldn't believe it. What trick is he pullin', I thought. But next day I find this guy Hedley's got guts. He's on the level. Not

113

gunnin' for us. He says to me . . . 'Look, Louie, you're runnin' scared. Bad scared. Why don'tcha come off it? For you know you're scared. But God loves you.'

" 'God loves me? Huh! That's a job,' I tell him. But he doesn't lay off. He sees right through me, and I begin to bawl. Just broke down and bawled. Strange thing happens then. Hedley puts his arm around me and says: 'I believe in you, Louie, because Jesus believes in you. You don't hafta run scared no more. You don't hafta run alone. For Jesus is pullin' for you. How about runnin' with Him?'

"I can't believe it! Me, the scared, the Kid, the Big Panther . . . bawlin'. Then I know. I'm nothin' . . . nothin' but a big scared kid. Afraid. Always runnin'. An' then it hit me. This Hedley was kinda like the Jesus-man who came to help the pushed-around people. And so I think if this guy can trust me, maybe God can love me and help me. 'Jesus, I'm gonna try to run with You. You gotta help me.'

"Wasn't easy. Specially that day I was walking home from the Center, and some of the old Panther guys stopped me. 'Quit us, because you got religion,' 'preacher's boy, Louie,' they start to yell. My fingers start to tighten up. Then I remember. I looked at my fists and dropped 'em. 'Look gang,' I said, 'I don't carry my knife anymore. Beat me up if you want. But I know how scared you're runnin'. I no longer runnin' scared. I found somethin'. This Jesus-man is no bluff. He's for real.' And the fellows begin to back off.

"Now three from the old Panther gang work down at the Center. . . . On Sundays we get together in a room at the Center to talk about the Jesus-man and how He helps us."

Rod

Rod's home is on Glenwood Street. Nice lawn here. Shade trees too. Rod and a couple of friends are out in the backyard for a game of touch football. Earlier in the day the family had gotten into the Chevrolet and had driven to church. Now Rod gets to do the driving!

Church—Rod has been going to church as long as he can re-

114

member . . . kindergarten, Bible school, junior and youth choirs, camp, youth fellowship. And this year Rod was in membership class. Just a month ago Rod was baptized.

Rod sometimes thinks of that moment when the minister put his hands on his head, and the water trickled down his neck. "Upon your profession of faith in the Lord Jesus Christ as your personal Savior from sin, and your vow of consecration to Him and His service, I baptize you. . . ."

Nothing so dramatic about it. But it was special. Rod can't remember when he didn't think of himself as a Christian. But he remembers the discussions at camp, and just sitting around the campfire thinking. Or that week before baptism he got up in front of his parents and friends in the church and said why he wanted to join the church. Rod does feel more sure that God loves him, and that he somehow belongs to God. Those problems that sometimes seemed so big, no longer seem quite as important. For he believes that God is concerned. And God forgives. Of that he is sure.

Oh, there still are a lot of things Rod doesn't understand (parents included, especially sometimes!). Sometimes he wonders about the church and the people in it. He has applied for a Servanthood Work Camp and looks forward to this chance to live and work together with other kids, and talk about their experiences and faith.

Nothing so dramatic. Rod can't pinpoint the day or time. But something has happened. His attitudes have changed—slowly, but surely; he has come to realize that his life is a gift. How will he use it? He feels part of something great and wonderful. He feels good about it.

CONVERSION—SUDDEN OR GRADUAL?

Some can remember the day and the hour when they came to Christ. Others can scarcely remember when they did not love Christ and try, with some earnestness, to follow Him. For some, the experience is sudden and dramatic, as with Paul. With others, the experience may be more like that of Timothy, who had a Christian mother and grandmother and who was nurtured in the Christian faith from an early age.

When the change comes in our lives, however, we must know that it has happened. We should know that our sins have been forgiven. Not to be able to point to any experience (or experiences) when God has called us to follow Him more closely and has drawn us to a new level of commitment and to a renewal of our desire to serve Him may mean that we have not yet experienced salvation.

We do not enter the kingdom without knowing it. True— our salvation was assured in A.D. 30. That was Moment I. But Moment II is also necessary, and that is when we accept what God has done for us in Christ, and believe that it was "for me."

STEPS IN BECOMING A CHRISTIAN

God takes the initiative and asserts the Christian faith. God's act in sending Jesus Christ, the life and death and resurrection of Jesus Christ, is an accomplished fact. And so we believe that in this act God has declared us "acceptable" and extended to us the forgiveness for our sin.

God has acted. But we are not puppets dangling at the end of strings wrapped around God's fingers. God does not control us

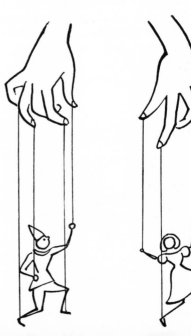

We are not puppets dangling at the end of strings wrapped around God's fingers.

mechanically. He does not push buttons. An important part of our understanding about God and man is that man has God-given freedoms to choose.

Philippians 2:12 reminds us to *work out your own salvation with fear and trembling.* What can we do? What must we do to be saved? Here are several steps that can help us.

1. *Recognize sin.* In Luke 15 we read the story of the prodigal, that young man who tried to make his own way. Because he deliberately turned his back on his father (God) Jesus spoke of him as being lost. The lost son did not come to his senses until he was hungry and had to take a job feeding pigs. When he saw that he lived no better than the pigs, he suddenly realized what had happened to his life; and he thought for the first time how good he had it in his father's house.

The first step in responding to God's offered salvation is to recognize that we need it. We need to recognize that without Christ, we are on the wrong track.

2. *Repent.* A man who gets on a train in Chicago and finds himself heading for New York when he really planned to go to Los Angeles would be foolish if he did nothing about it. But he could realize that he was on the wrong train and still wind up in New York.

Recognizing his mistake is not enough. He must do something about it. It is not enough to recognize our sin. We have to do something about it. The Bible's word is repent. It means "turn" or "return." Repentance is not simply being sorry. It is not merely the desire to go in the other direction. Repentance is getting off the wrong train and taking the right one.

The prodigal son not only recognized the mess he had gotten himself into, but said to himself, *"I will arise and go to my father, and I will say to him, 'Father, I have sinned . . .'* (Lk. 15:18). He not only determined to go home, he went home.

Repentance involves confession and the making right of things wherever possible. The restoring of broken relations with people is necessary for healing. The Lord's Prayer emphasizes this, "Forgive us our debts, we forgiving our debtors" (Mt. 6:12 Buttrick).

117

3. *Accept God's forgiveness in Christ.* Our part in salvation? We must recognize our need. We must repent. Most important of all, we must accept God's forgiveness in Christ.

Forgiveness is a gift. It is not earned. The lost son who returned home had no claim to his father's love and home anymore. But the father's arm went around the son's shoulders nevertheless, and there was rejoicing for both father and son.

Accepting Christ is accepting God's forgiving love. It is also accepting Jesus Christ as a new center for our lives. We give up the independence and self-centeredness that can only lead us down the wrong track, and become centered in Christ.

HOW CAN I BE SURE?

"Sometimes I feel really close to God and then I think I am a Christian. But then when I have done wrong I feel so far away from God. How can you be sure you are a Christian or not?"

How can we know? We are sure only because God said so. He has promised this. Evidence that this salvation has become ours, and is still becoming ours includes:

> Deliverance from our own self-will, our self-centeredness, our self-conscious fears and worries;
> Yielding ourselves to God's will for us, and knowing His forgiveness for what we have done wrong;
> Finding our greatest joy in a closer fellowship with God, and with other people;
> And a resultant happiness which the ups and downs of life can't touch.[30]

This doesn't usually happen all at once. Becoming a Christian is the beginning of growth in a new way of life. Also, we need to remember that God doesn't stop loving us when we do wrong. There is nothing we can do which will make God stop loving us.

What evidence do you see in your own life that helps you to know you are a Christian?

WORDS TO REMEMBER

Repent. To turn; to feel sorry for wrongdoing, and to change our life.

118

Conversion. Change in belief or conviction; turning from a sinful to a new way of life.

Believe. To trust; to stake one's life on Jesus Christ.

Christian. Follower of Christ; one who accepts Christ as his Savior and Lord, and commits himself to follow and serve Him.

CHRIST AND YOUR LIFE

1. What steps do *you* need to take to become a Christian or to grow in your Christian life?

2. How can a person actually receive Christ into his life? Do Jesus' words in Matthew 5:6, or Paul's words in Romans 10: 9-13, help you in any way?

3. Have you ever asked Jesus Christ to come into your life with His forgiveness and love and controlling purpose? You can do it in your own words, or a prayer like: "Lord, I thank You for dying for me, and I now ask You to come into my life as my Savior. I want to follow You without reservation."

4. If you are troubled about becoming a Christian, and have questions about it, this would be a good time to talk about it with someone you trust. Or if this decision to be a follower of Christ has already been made, you will find it helpful to speak with someone about it, a close friend, your parents, or your pastor. Your pastor will help you make plans for the day when you make this profession of faith public, and for your baptism into the church of Christ.

30. Nevin C. Harner, *I Believe* (Philadelphia: United Church, 1950), p. 111.

Chapter 16

What Is the Church?

For just as the body is one and has many members, and all the members of the body, though many, are one body, so it is with Christ. For by one Spirit we were all baptized into one body. . . . Now you are the body of Christ and individually members of it.
1 Corinthians 12:12, 13, 27

Among the world's classic fiction stories is Daniel Defoe's *Robinson Crusoe,* written in 1719. Crusoe, shipwrecked and finding himself alone on an island, pits his wits against the raw forces of nature. All by himself, he builds his own little kingdom on that island.

Written today, that story might be about a rocket shipwreck on some unknown, desolate planet or satellite. Our Robinson Crusoe would use his superior intelligence and ingenuity not only to survive, but to build himself a king's life on this hurtling space island.

But, "No man is an island, entire of itself, every man is a piece of the continent, a part of the main. . . ," wrote poet John Donne. Certainly no Christian can be an island, living by himself or for himself alone. In our definition of a Christian, we said, "A Christian is one who responds to the call of Christ."

But Christ's call seldom if ever, comes apart from the church. So our response to Christ includes also commitment to the church of Christ.

How important is it that you be a member of the church? What is the church? What is the church's purpose and power?

THAT WORD: CHURCH

What ideas come to your mind when you think of the word *church*?

120

Every man is part of the main. . . .

Many of our experiences with the church center in a building. Church buildings are important. But the Christian church did not have buildings in which to worship until a hundred or more years after Christ. Even today there are church groups like the Amish who meet in homes for worship. So we must look elsewhere, beyond a building, for a description of the church.

The word *church* as used in the New Testament translates a Greek word, *ekklesia. Ekklesia* means an assembly of people. Tracing the use of this word back to the Greek translation of the Old Testament, we find it used to translate two Hebrew words. One meant a company assembled by appointment. The other referred to a community called together for counsel or action.

The word *ekklesia* identifies the church as the people of God in the same stream as God's faithful in the Old Testament and before Pentecost. As the people of God were gathered together by God's mighty acts in Egypt and Sinai, so the new people of God were called into being by God's mighty acts in Jesus Christ.

The idea of *ekklesia* is not one of being called out of the world, of withdrawal from the world. Rather, the church is the people of God called to declare God's purpose to the world and to minister in the world.

THE CHURCH: THE BODY OF CHRIST

The New Testament uses the analogy of the human body to describe the church. A body has many parts: eyes, ears, nose, arms, legs, stomach, and lungs. Each of these parts is needed. Each has a specific task that contributes to the working of the whole body. And each is dependent upon the source of life.

For it is in Christ that the complete Godhead dwells embodied, and in him you have been brought to completion (Col. 2:9 NEB). God acted in Christ. In Christ's coming and giving of himself for us, we become one with Him, in order that we may do His work upon the earth.

Read 1 Corinthians 12:12-27 to help you think of the church as "the body of Christ." What does this say to you about the church needing you? What does it say about commitment to the church?

Pastor Herbert Reich tells this story. Workers were putting finishing touches to the new church building when a visitor came into the sanctuary to watch. The painters were just completing the last wall. There a workman hung a lamp; here final squares of flooring were fitted into place. In the back the pews were being set down. The church would soon be ready.

As the visitor looked around, he seemed quite satisfied with what he saw. But then he cast his glance on the long high wall above the altar, where a large picture of the Good Shepherd was being painted. He couldn't see much yet—only firm brush strokes outlining the head and shoulders of Christ, and a long shepherd's staff; that was about all.

Turning to a worker, the visitor asked, "When will this picture be finished?"

"That picture," said the worker, "is finished."

"What do you mean, 'finished'? Most of it is still missing—the hands, feet, mouth, arms, legs—in fact, the whole body is missing!"

"You won't see that on the wall," the workman said. "The body of Christ is the congregation of people who will be worshiping here in this church." The body of Christ is the church!

THE CHURCH: A HOLY COMMUNITY

Another important New Testament word referring to the church is *koinonia*. It means fellowship, sharing, partnership.

Members of the Christian community are all sons of a common Father. All share in an undivided Christ, and an undivided Spirit. All are members one of another, participating in this life with each other.

Obviously, this is something deeper than the popular understanding of fellowship as "a good time and a good feeling." We are "members one of another."

Believers in Christ do not decide to *have* fellowship. They *are* a community. And this Christian community is created and sustained by the awareness of a common body of beliefs, a common life in Christ, a common commitment to Him in faith and obedience, and a common expression of Christian love. *Koinonia* comes about when we become responsible to each other and for each other.

Read Acts 2:42-47 for a description of the early Christian community. What characteristics of the church are mentioned here? What were the results of this kind of participation together in life? Does this describe the kind of church you know? If not, what do you feel is wrong?

THE CHURCH: POWERED BY THE SPIRIT

Is the church the people of God, Christ's body on earth? Is the church the Christian community in which people actually participate in Christ's life and become responsible to each other?

> "Hold on! Are you trying to say that the church actually makes a difference? From what I see it doesn't matter much whether you belong to church or not. Most people are about the same, I guess, except for the real squares, and they're so different they don't count. If the church would ever get around to doing anything that means something . . . instead of just sitting on religion all the time. . . ."

In spite of all the imperfections of the church, in spite of jealousy, division, complacency, and indifference, we know that the church continues. And the Spirit continues to change and move thousands of men and women today. For many there is a devotion to Christ that is no less than that of the early Christians we read about in the Book of Acts.

To understand the church at all we need to catch a glimpse of the dynamic power that created the church. For even though ignored and misunderstood the Holy Spirit is still at work.

The Acts of the Apostles has sometimes been called the Acts of the Holy Spirit, for it is the story of the Spirit of God moving mightily in the lives of a group of faithful men and women who came to be referred to as those who "have turned the world upside down" (Acts 17:6).

In chapter 14, we looked at the church as a result of the resurrection. The disciples of Jesus did not just kid themselves into believing Jesus' living presence was there. To them, His Living Spirit *was* there, even as He had promised.

That promise is recorded in detail in John 14-16. It was Jesus' last meal with His twelve disciples. Jesus was preparing His closest friends for His going away. He knew what the crucifixion would mean for Him, and also what it would mean for His disciples. They will be scattered. They will be persecuted. They, too, may face a martyr's death. They will be afraid.

The word Jesus uses to describe the Spirit is *paraclete*. This is translated "comforter" (KJV), "counselor" (RSV), "helper" (Williams), "Advocate" (NEB). The Counselor will come, says Jesus, so that we will not have to stand alone. He will be with us in life and whatever is to come upon us.

Acts 2 then tells the story of Pentecost—the shaking up and filling of these disciples with the boldness of Christ's presence— and how the Spirit bound them into a fellowship. Here was the community of the Holy Spirit, the church, the Spirit-filled community. For God was at work in and through the lives of these believers.

Read Acts 4:8-12, 18:35 aloud to catch the excitement of this new dynamic power surging through the fellowship of believers.

THE HOLY SPIRIT, THE CHURCH, AND YOU

A sundial is a device with angles and numbers properly arranged so that it will tell the correct time of day as the sun moves across the daytime sky. The dial may be properly constructed and set up. But it stands as a useless piece of junk, unless the sun shines on it.

No matter how wonderful our life might be, it may not count. To be useful and meaningful, our lives must be placed where

God's Spirit may illumine and empower and use them. The Apostle Paul, out of personal experience, declared, *the Lord is the Spirit, and where the Spirit of the Lord is, there is freedom* (2 Cor. 3:17).

Freedom to become what we are meant to be! Freedom to use the gifts that are truly ours! And where is this freedom and this power found? Jesus said, *"Where two or three are gathered in my name, there am I in the midst of them"* (Mt. 18:20).

How does God's Spirit work in our lives through the church?

1. *He convicts us of sin.* Human nature is basically selfish. We are adept at building little fences around our "self." It takes a power from outside ourselves to show us what we really are and can become. The Spirit convicts us of sin by showing us our poverty of spirit as we see the holiness of God. In true worship this can happen.

2. *He makes God's love real.* The Holy Spirit plays an important part in conversion. Without that stirring inside us, that pricking of our soul, we would not be ready to get off "the wrong train" and onto "the right train." When Saul of Tarsus headed for Damascus to persecute the Christians, it was the Holy Spirit that worked in him, calling him to halt and face God in all His holy judgment and mercy. When Saul responded, the love of God through Jesus Christ became real to him. Later Paul wrote of it, *God's love has been poured into our hearts through the Holy Spirit which has been given to us* (Rom. 5:5). This was the very assurance a frustrated Saul of Tarsus needed. Never forget, however, that the encouragement of an Ananias and a Barnabas was also part of the Spirit's work in Paul's life.

3. *He nurtures the Christian's life.* Paul, in writing to the Galatians, points out how *the fruit of the Spirit is love, joy, peace, patience, kindness, goodness, faithfulness, gentleness, self-control* (Galatians 5:22, 23). The person who is not under the control of the Spirit finds himself involved in the work of the flesh: *immorality, impurity, licentiousness, idolatry, sorcery, enmity, strife, jealousy, anger, selfishness, dissension, party spirit, envy,*

drunkenness, carousing . . . (Gal. 5:19-21). In other words, if you are not under the control of the Spirit of God, you are a slave to yourself and selfish desires.

4. *He brings power.* From fearful, disillusioned, weak disciples, the early Christians became a band of fearless convinced missionaries! Jesus had promised at the ascension, *"You shall receive power when the Holy Spirit has come upon you"* (Acts 1:8). Through the Spirit's power, they became witnesses, spreading the message of the living Christ through Jerusalem, throughout all Palestine, and unto the ends of the earth!

5. *He is our guide.* Here is direction, not just movement or blind force. Luke tells us in Acts that it was in the worshiping church that the Holy Spirit spoke, *"Set apart for me Barnabas and Saul for the work to which I have called them"* (Acts 13:2). Again Luke tells how the Spirit led Paul on his mission journeys, informing Paul when to go and when not to go (Acts 16:6-10).

WORDS TO REMEMBER

Church. Building set aside for worship; a congregation; a body of believers holding the same creed and following the same practices; the fellowship of all believers in Christ.

Koinonia. Fellowship in the sense of sharing, participating.

Holy Spirit. God in action. The form in which God makes His living presence felt to guide us and empower us.

THE SPIRIT IN LIFE TODAY

1. Discuss this definition. "Believers in Jesus Christ, gathered in fellowship for worship, study, and service, are the church." Does this mean that when any of these three activities is omitted, that we do not have the church? That people who come only to Sunday worship may not really be the church? That people who do not come at all are not really in the church at all? That a name on a church roll doesn't mean a thing?

2. In what ways is the Spirit of God at work today? Where can you see the Spirit working in situations of racial conflict or war between nations? Or is the Spirit powerless here?

3. Have you seen anything of the Spirit's work in the lives of persons you know? Where have you felt the movements of God's Spirit in your life? Or if not, what steps do you need to take to open your life to God's Spirit?

A PRAYER FOR THE CHURCH

O Eternal God, who by thy Son Jesus Christ didst establish
 the family of thy Church in all the world,
breathe upon it anew the gifts of thy Holy Spirit,
 that, awakening to thy command,
it may go forth in lowly service, yet in conquering might,
 to win mankind to the love of thy Name;
through Jesus Christ. Amen.[31]

31. *The Pastor's Prayer Book,* ed. Robert N. Rodenmayer (New York: Oxford University Press, 1960), p. 170.

Chapter 17

The Church's Story

Jesus: *"Who do you say that I am?"*

Peter: *"You are the Christ, the Son of the living God."*

Jesus: *". . . And I tell you, you are Peter, and on this rock I will build my church, and the powers of death shall not prevail against it. I will give you the keys of the kingdom of heaven. . . . Matthew 16:15-19.*

"But you shall receive power when the Holy Spirit has come upon you; and you shall be my witnesses in Jerusalem and in all Judea and Samaria and to the end of the earth." Acts 1:8

Sometimes we forget that the church has been around for a long time. We may get impatient with what we see of the church. We may feel it no longer speaks to the needs of a space age. We may wonder whether the church is about washed up.

But no understanding of the church is adequate without at least some knowledge of its story—the beginnings, the amazing growth, the struggles, the agony of its failures, the fresh thrusts of the Spirit, and the ideals and hope still alive after nearly twenty centuries.

At the very heart of the church's story is the belief that God has called the church into existence. God in His love is seeking to win sinful man back to himself. By calling the church, He is working through a particular group of people who have faith in Him, and through them the peoples of the world can come to know His love.

THE NEW TESTAMENT CHURCH, A.D. 30-100

The church began with Jesus. He gathered about Him a group of disciples. Their lives were changed by Him. He taught them the love and way of God. On Pentecost, fifty days after the resurrection, the Holy Spirit came upon them. They knew that the God whom they had seen so clearly in Jesus was still present with them giving them understanding and boldness. They were beside themselves with joy, and many were added to the fellowship of believers in Jesus Christ on that day.

At first the Christians attended the Jewish temple daily. They also gathered in Christian homes for breaking bread, praising God, listening to the apostles' teachings about Jesus, and praying (Acts 2:42, 46). There was no special organization except that the twelve apostles did most of the preaching and teaching. Deacons were appointed to help in distributing the food and goods they shared.

Soon Jewish persecution drove them from the temple, and even for a time from Jerusalem. They began to preach in Samaria. Then after the remarkable conversion of Paul, the message spread further. The Jerusalem council, A.D. 50, (See Acts 15.) ruled that becoming a Christian did not require becoming a Jew first. Now the faith was spread throughout the Mediterranean world.

PERSECUTION AND GROWTH, A.D. 70-313

For some years Jerusalem remained the center of church life. But when that city was destroyed by the Romans in the year A.D. 70, new centers of Christian influence developed—Antioch, Ephesus, and Rome.

By A.D. 250 the church had believers and an organization that stretched from southern France to the Tigris and Euphrates Valley in Asia. Across northern Africa half the people were Christians. A letter written about the church at Rome tells of 30,000 church members in that city!

During those first three centuries the Roman government tried again and again to destroy the Christian faith and all Christians. Although many weakened under persecution, the persistent testimony of the "Christ ones" who died for their faith proved the Christian faith stronger than the Roman Empire. The result was that many more joined the church and made a confession that "Jesus is Lord."

THE RELIGION OF A MIGHTY EMPIRE, A.D. 313-500

The persecutions came to an end with Constantine, A.D. 313. The story is that in a battle near Rome on October 23, 312, Constantine saw a cross in the skies with the words (in Latin), "In this sign conquer." Victorious in his drive to become Emperor of Rome, Constantine inaugurated religious liberty. Christianity was put on a level with any other religion of the empire. The cross was stamped on Roman coins. The "Lord's Day" of the Christians was made a legal holiday. Now it was a simple step for Christianity to become *the* religion of the Roman Empire. At last it was easy to be a Christian, perhaps too easy.

Moving from the faith of a tiny group of Jews to the religion of a mighty empire changed the church. Differences in belief and action were reflected in the church. Various new offices became necessary—pastors, prophets, teachers, bishops, and elders. Since Rome was the capital city of the empire, the bishop of Rome came to be looked upon as having final authority. He became known as "pope" (from the Latin word *papa,* "father").

The church faced many problems. Was Christ a ghost or a real man? What should happen to Christians who deserted in persecution and then wanted to come back when times were better? Constantine called three hundred bishops together at Nicaea (near Constantinople) in the year 325. Out of this first great council at Nicaea the Nicene Creed was developed as a statement of belief about Jesus and His relationship to God.

As for people whose faith had wavered, a system of "confession" (first to the congregation, later to a priest only) and "penance" (made-up penalty for sin) was worked out.

Among the brilliant thinkers and writers of this time was Augustine of Hippo. *The City of God* is one of his books about the church as the company of God's faithful people. In 476, not many years after Augustine's death, the city of Rome was de-

131

stroyed. But the church was greater than Rome. The "City of God" was strong, and becoming stronger.

CENTURIES OF DARKNESS AND LIGHT, A.D. 500-1500

The union of church and empire both helped and hindered the church. The influence of Christian kings spread the faith, but it also diluted the faith. When the French King Clovis was baptized in 496, he in turn had his entire army and kingdom baptized. The church spread to England, across the European continent, touched the Scandinavian countries, and Russia by the tenth century.

When the Pope crowned Charlemagne Emperor in A.D. 800, church and state became the Holy Roman Empire. More than ever before the church and state were locked in a battle against the followers of the prophet Mohammed, Islam. The Turks, believers in Islam, had conquered the Holy Land. From 1096-1272 a series of Christian Crusades (holy wars) were carried out in which thousands were killed.

The church had become very powerful. Many people had given their land to the church, and it became the most powerful landowner in every kingdom. No one could be king without the Pope's permission. On one occasion, because of a dispute about appointing bishops, Pope Gregory VII ruled that King Henry IV of England was no longer in the church and all his subjects could rebel against him. So desperate was the king's plight that he traveled to northern Italy and stood outside the Pope's castle gate three days in his bare feet in the cold of winter to show his penitence.

But power can corrupt. Sometimes the power of the pope's position made it a prize for evil men. The church's history has many stories of things done in the name of the church for which Christians can only feel a deep shame. In 1054 the church was split with another pope claiming to be the true pope, this time in Constantinople. From this tradition the Greek, Russian, and Syrian churches have descended.

Yet many devout persons sought to keep alive a deep understanding of the teachings of Christ. Some of them, disgusted with the worldliness of the church, turned their backs on normal life and became monks or nuns, giving up all the possessions, promising not to marry, and promising to abide by a series of disciplines. They were organized into "orders," usually as followers of some great leader like Augustine, Francis, Dominic, and others. An early monk, Jerome, had translated the Bible into Latin, making it available to the church for centuries to come.

Sometimes groups who criticized the church were put out of the church as the Waldensians were in 1179. John Wycliffe of England wanted the priests to let the people read the Bible. John Huss preached the same in Bohemia. He criticized the Roman Catholic Church for selling "indulgences," "the stored-up-goodness" of Christ, and the saints that could be purchased for money. The church burned John Huss at the stake. But the new ideas that were stirring could not be burned.

The church's history has many stories of things done in the name of the church. . . .

THE PROTESTANT REFORMATION, A.D. 1500-1600

Martin Luther had been a monk in the Roman Catholic Church. But as he studied the Bible he became convinced that men are not saved by their good deeds, but by God's gracious love. When John Tetzel came to Germany to sell indulgences and said that as soon as the money hit the collection box some soul would be saved, Luther drew up a list of nintey-five statements which he was willing to debate with the Catholic Church. On October 31, 1517, he nailed the list on the church door at Wittenberg.

Luther, at first, had no intention of leaving the Catholic Church. He only wished to reform it. Four years later, when he was called on to recant his writings, he refused. "Here I stand; I cannot do otherwise; God help me." On the way home from the trial, friends kidnapped him—for his own protection. In hiding, he translated the Bible into the German language. In Germany, the churches that broke away from the Roman Catholic Church came to be known as the Lutheran Church.

In German Switzerland, Ulrich Zwingli was as eager as Martin Luther for the church to go back to early Christian beliefs. His followers came to be known as the Reformed. Other leaders of this group were John Calvin in French Switzerland and John Knox in Scotland.

THE REFORMATION AND THE MENNONITES

There were others who agreed with Luther and Zwingli and Calvin that Jesus Christ is the only sufficient Savior. But they did not feel these men had gone far enough in their reforms.

Among these were the Swiss Brethren from whom our church traditions stem. In Zurich, these men included Conrad Grebel, the son of a wealthy family; Felix Manz, a university-trained student of the Hebrew language, and George Blaurock (blue coat—for the color of his robe), a former priest.

As these men studied the Bible, they became concerned that those who claimed to be a part of the church knew nothing of a serious effort to live a new life. Searching the Scriptures, they discovered no evidence for infant baptism and the idea that everyone in a particular geographical area is automatically a church member. Rather, they came to believe that a church should be made up of those few who wish by their own decision to join the fellowship and earnestly seek to live a new life. This new church, they felt, must not be connected with the government so that anyone who chooses may be free to join but no one is forced to against his will.

When several of the "brethren" refused to have their children baptized, Zwingli and the Council of Zurich opposed the group.

On January 21, 1525, Grebel baptized Blaurock who in turn baptized several others. That was the birth of the "over-again baptizers," the Anabaptists, as they were called by their enemies. As their numbers grew, so did persecution. In 1527 Felix Manz was drowned for his beliefs. By 1531 most of the Anabaptists were eliminated from the Zurich area. Many had fled north, and their ideas spread to Germany, France, and Holland.

These "brethren" would rather sacrifice their lives and property than to violate Christ's commandment "to love one another." Menno Simons, a converted Catholic priest from Witmarsum, became the guiding spirit of the Dutch Anabaptists. The peaceful Anabaptists came to be known as the followers of Menno—Mennonists—and finally Mennonites.

POST-REFORMATION, AFTER A.D. 1600

An outline of the church's story during these recent centuries includes:

> Development of the Anglican Church in England (Episcopal in the United States)
>
> The church comes to America and follows the frontier, (Congregationalists, Quakers, Moravians, Mennonites, Brethren, and many other Christian groups)
>
> The rapid growth of Methodism and the Baptist movement
>
> Continual dividing until there are over 200 Protestant denominations
>
> Revivals, Sunday schools, colleges, hospitals

The great mission movement during the nineteenth and twentieth centuries and the organization of national churches as the fruit of this missionary work

Involvement in social reforms like the industrial and racial revolutions, peace witness in an atomic age, and concern with the problems of poverty

Movements toward cooperation, and a spirit of unity in Christendom, as symbolized by organization of a World Council of Churches at Amsterdam in 1948

New efforts to discover the mission of the church in a world becoming urban, and to find new forms the church can take to minister to the world's needs today.

This is the church's story in part—some of the good and some of the bad. The church reaches back into the past to Jesus himself. Wherever people live the church has gone. And into a changing future, we believe the church will continue to move.

The church, as the people of God, is the continuing incarnation of Jesus Christ in God's reconciling mission to the world. Always, the church is in danger of slipping to the level of routine and organization. Always there is the temptation to confuse Christianity with the culture of the day. Always there is need for revival and renewal. What will be your part in helping to shape the church of today and tomorrow?

WORDS TO REMEMBER

Catholic. Universal; the word can be applied to the whole Christian church, though commonly the word is used as referring to members of the Roman Catholic Church.

Congregation. A group of believers who meet in a specific place for worship, study, fellowship, and service.

Denomination. A church body made up of congregations that have the same beliefs and the same type of church government.

Ecumenical. Worldwide, a word often applied to the unity of the church.

Reformation. The religious movement of the sixteenth century which sought to bring new life into the church, and resulted in the formation of the Protestant churches.

THE CHURCH IN YOUR COMMUNITY

1. What churches are represented in your community? Find out what beliefs and practices they have in common. What differences are there?

2. When and how did the Mennonite church come into being? A summary of the development of our church can be found in the *Mennonite Encyclopedia* articles "Mennonite Church" and "General Conference Mennonite Church."

3. When, why, and how did the church you attend come into being? What seems to be the main purpose and mission of the church fellowship you know best?

OUR PRAYER FOR THE CHURCH

O God, give to the church a new vision and a new charity, a new wisdom and fresh understanding, the revival of her brightness and the renewal of her unity; that the eternal message of Thy Son, undefiled by the traditions of men, may be hailed as the good news of the new age; through Him who makes all things new, Jesus Christ our Lord.[32]

32. Percy Dearmer, *The Pastor's Prayer Book,* ed. Robert N. Rodenmayer (New York: Oxford University Press, 1960), p. 198.

Chapter 18

Baptism -- Witness to Faith

> *There is one body and one Spirit . . . one Lord, one*
> *faith, one baptism . . .* Ephesians 4:4, 5
> *Do you not know that all of us who have been*
> *baptized into Christ Jesus were baptized into his*
> *death? We were buried therefore with him by baptism into*
> *death, so that as Christ was raised from the dead*
> *by the glory of the Father, we too might walk in*
> *newness of life.* Romans 6:3, 4

TWENTY CENTURIES OF BAPTISM

Act 1

Time: A.D. 51

Place: Philippi, Macedonia (now Greece)

Scene: A nighttime celebration in the house of the city jailer.

A strange night, this. The jailer had already gone to bed when an earthquake rocked the prison. Locks snapped, doors flung open, the stocks were torn loose! Losing his head at the idea of all the prisoners escaping, the jailer intended to take his own life. Then he heard Paul's strong, calm, "We are all here."

In that moment, in Paul's words and in Paul's voice, the jailer recognized something he could not claim. Here was an untroubled confidence that the jailer did not have, and could not understand. Trembling with fear, he sank to the floor at Paul and Silas' feet, and blurted out his question: *"What must I do to be saved?"*

Here was a broken and humbled man, facing reality for the first time, facing his deepest need for a faith. Then came the reassuring words of these strangely wonderful men, *"Believe in the Lord Jesus, and you will be saved."* Commitment. And then, baptism into the name of Jesus.

This was a night to celebrate! A new confidence, a new direction, and a new joy had come to life! (Acts 16:25-34).

Act 2

    Time: A.D. 1531

    Place: Pingjum, Friesland (now the Netherlands)

    Scene: Menno Simons, a young Catholic priest, is seated at his writing table. His New Testament lies open at Romans 6.

Menno's eyes are closed in thought. He cannot shake the image that keeps coming back to trouble his mind. It is the image of Sicke Freerks, the honest and quiet tailor from the neighboring village of Leeuwarden.

Again Menno's mind sees Freerks. Freerks has just been condemned to death. Beheaded, his body is tied to the wheel, and his head put on a pole. His offense: baptism as an adult, because he believed faith necessary for the act of baptism.

Why? Why should a man die for such a belief? Slowly his hand moves toward the quill, and he begins to write in the journal on the table . . . "Still it sounds strange . . . a second baptism . . . yet I have examined the Scriptures carefully and meditated on them earnestly, but find nothing in them concerning infant baptism. . . ."[33]

Act 3

    Time: Twentieth century

    Place: First Mennonite Church, Anytown, U.S.A.

    Scene: Seven young people are kneeling at the front of the sanctuary.

Slowly Pastor Benton moves from one person to the next. Each time he dips his hands in a basin held by one of the deacons, and with his cupped hands pours a little water on the bowed head.

Placing his hand gently on the head, he says slowly, deliberately, "Upon your profession of faith in the Lord Jesus Christ as your personal Savior from sin, and your vow of consecration to Him and His service, I baptize you in the name of the Father, and of the Son, and of the Holy Spirit. May the Lord indeed baptize you with His Spirit from above."

Ruth feels Pastor Benton's hand slowly lift as he moves on to Jim. "Now you are washed . . . now, a member of Christ's church!" she thinks. "O God," she prays in the silence, "help me to know what this means."

QUESTIONS ABOUT BAPTISM

What does baptism mean? How necessary is it? Does one become a Christian by receiving baptism? Is there something about this rite that actually changes us? Or is baptism simply the act which leads to membership in the church? Is that all there is to it?

Why do some churches baptize babies, and others insist that only adults should be baptized? Why is water used, and why do some churches "pour" and others "immerse"? What are the requirements for baptism?

BAPTISM: SACRAMENT OR ORDINANCE?

In the life and worship of the church, certain acts have a very special significance. Baptism is one of these acts often referred to as a sacrament or ordinance. Though churches have not always agreed about which acts belong to this category, all the churches that have sacraments or ordinances agree that baptism is one of them.

The word *sacrament* emphasizes the mystery of God's grace in the life of the believer. Augustine, an early Christian writer, referred to a sacrament as "the visible form of an invisible grace." Thomas Aquinas, the famous Catholic theologian, referred to it as "the sign of a sacred thing in so far as it sanctifies man."

But this became one of the problems. Too much emphasis on the "sign" and "the visible form," made people think of the sacraments as having a magical effect. So it came about that people were driven through the water in masses, to be "saved." Babies were brought for baptism, lest they die before the sacred water assured their salvation. And for a time, baptism was even deferred until just before death. That way every last sin might be "washed away" by the water before a person died.

The Reformers of the sixteenth century rejected the magical concept of the sacraments. Though the Lutheran and Anglican churches kept a meaning of sacrament that emphasized God's grace, other reformers saw these acts as symbols. In baptism and the Lord's Supper, they said, we act out a spiritual meaning.

The Anabaptists came to call these acts instituted or commanded by Jesus, ordinances. They believed Jesus commanded these acts for His followers as a way of remembering His death and resurrection, and of identifying with Him. They also believed the value of these ordinances depended upon the faith the believer brought to them. What led them to this view? Is this still a valid conclusion?

INFANT OR ADULT BAPTISM?

The earliest Anabaptist statement of faith begins with this article on baptism.

> "First. Observe concerning baptism: Baptism shall be given to all those who have learned repentance and amendment of life, and who believe truly that their sins are taken away by Christ, and to all those who walk in the resurrection of Jesus Christ, and wish to be buried with Him in death, so that they may be resurrected with Him, and to all those who with this significance request it (baptism) of us and demand it for themselves. This excludes all infant baptism, the highest and chief abomination of the pope. In this you have the foundation and testimony of the apostles. Matthew 28, Mark 16, Acts 2, 8, 16, 19. This we wish to hold simply, yet firmly and with assurance" (Schleitheim Confession of 1527).

Study of the Scriptures led Anabaptists to this view. Nowhere in the Bible did they find support for the common practice of baptizing infants. Instead, they found baptism related to repentance (Acts 2:38) and with the faith and commitment of the believer (Acts 8:12, 35-38).

Defenders of infant baptism have referred to Acts 16:15 and 33, and 1 Corinthians 1:16, passages about baptism of a family or household. This they believe included the children. Others have tried to identify baptism with the Jewish act of circumcision. But circumcision was an act only for Jewish boy babies.

Irenaeus, living more than one hundred years after Christ, is the first church teacher who specifically refers to baptizing infants.

In spite of the fact that infant baptism is based largely on the tradition of the church, many Protestant churches have kept the practice. Martin Luther recognized the relationship of faith to baptism, but spoke of a child's "hidden faith." Churches practicing infant baptism emphasize God's grace to the child. Children are part of the covenant too.

In infant baptism, the child is dedicated to the Lord by parents and sponsors. The parents and the church are saying, "We will be faithful in the nurture of this child." Some of our churches have a parent-child dedication service to emphasize the responsibility of Christian parents. And most of the churches that practice infant baptism have a confirmation service. Confirmation is a public confession of faith in Jesus Christ as Savior and Lord, and the act of being received by the church into active membership. In this sense it is much like our catechism preparation which climaxes in baptism and reception into the church.

BAPTISM BY IMMERSION OR POURING?

How shall I be baptized? Does it make any difference? Is there only one correct way?

The forms used are immersion, in which the person enters and is covered by the water, or pouring (also sprinkling) in which only a small amount of water is placed on the applicant's head.

The arguments in favor of immersion include:

1. Early meanings of the word *baptism* include to dip or to immerse.

2. John baptized where there was much water and in the Jordan.

3. The illustration Paul uses in Romans 6 of the believer dying and rising with Christ seems especially appropriate when one thinks of immersion.

4. Early church writings like the *Teaching of the Twelve Apostles* hint at immersion. Many historians think immersion was the usual practice.

Arguments in favor of sprinkling or pouring include:

1. The word *baptism* also has other meanings than to dip or immerse. It is used of washing and cleansing acts.

2. To speak of John baptizing *in* the Jordan may mean only geographical location.

3. Romans 6 emphasizes the believer's death to sin and renewal in righteousness rather than a form of baptism.

4. Early church writings also refer to pouring.

We must conclude that both forms were used from earliest times. To argue for the validity of one at the expense of the other is to miss the point of baptism.[34]

Pouring is the form used most commonly in the Mennonite church. The emphasis has been on inward meanings rather than outward forms. So our church has recognized other forms also. The symbol is of less importance than that which it symbolizes. What matters most is not that a person has been voluntarily baptized by immersion or by pouring. More important is that a person has died with Christ and has been raised again to newness of life in Him, so that his life is now hid with Christ in God (Rom. 6:3-11).

WHAT BAPTISM CAN MEAN

In *My Christian Faith,* the significance of baptism is described as a sign:

of inward cleansing,
  of the death of our inward self,
    of putting on Christ,
      of uniting with His church,
        of entering into a covenant with our Lord,
          and of receiving the Holy Spirit" (p. 32).

In baptism we identify ourselves with Christ in His death and resurrection. This involves saying No to an old way of life, so

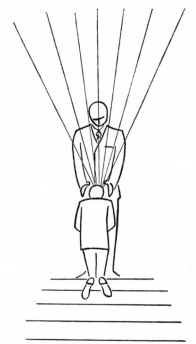

Baptism is our conscious, deliberate, public identification with God and His people.

that we may say Yes to the new kind of life which has its source in Christ.

But baptism is never a private vow. It is our conscious, deliberate, public identification with God and His people. To die to oneself is to *leave* oneself. But no one can leave himself unless he has somewhere else to go! In baptism we cast our lot with the *community of the Spirit,* and God's mission for the whole world through the church. We enter into a new relationship with God and man in which life is seen in terms of living for others.

Baptism is a beginning, the beginning of a new adventure— a life of consecrated discipleship.

WORDS TO REMEMBER

Sacrament. A religious ceremony instituted or commanded by Christ. Since sacrament came to emphasize the mysteriousness of

God's grace to the believer, and took on magical meanings for many, our church has preferred to call baptism and the Lord's Supper ordinances.

Baptism. The ordinance of the church by which an individual publicly witnesses to his faith in Jesus Christ as his personal Savior and pledges his life to Him in obedience and is received into the fellowship of the church.

Confirmation. The act in which a person who has been baptized as a child confirms his parents' promises and expresses his own faith and is admitted to the full responsibilities and privileges of church membership.

YOUR BAPTISM

1. Why do you wish to be baptized, or why do you hesitate?
2. What do you expect of a member of Christ's church?
3. As you consider baptism, what commitments do you plan to make?
4. In what ways will you try to keep the act and meaning of baptism alive in your life?

A PRAYER BEFORE BAPTISM

Dear God, I thank You that I have found out about You from my parents and from my pastors and teachers. I am glad I know that You love me and accept me as Your child.

For the knowledge that You forgive my sins, for faith in my Savior Jesus, for the new excitement of trusting in Your Spirit, I thank You.

I am sorry that I do not always think and talk and act like a Christian. But I am glad I am a Christian, and I want Your Holy Spirit to strengthen me in my faith. For I want my life to count for You. Amen.

33. J. C. Wenger, editor, *The Complete Writings of Menno Simons* (Scottdale: Herald Press, 1966), p. 7.

34. Henry Poettcker, *A Study on Baptism* (Newton, Kansas: Faith and Life Press, 1963), pp. 12-15.

Chapter 19

The Lord's Supper

. . . the Lord Jesus on the night when he was betrayed took bread, and when he had given thanks, he broke it, and said, "This is my body which is for you. Do this in remembrance of me." In the same way also the cup, after supper, saying, "This cup is the new covenant in my blood. Do this, as often as you drink it, in remembrance of me. 1 Corinthians 11:23b-25

EATING AND DRINKING AND REMEMBERING!

On Passover Eve the Jewish family gathers around the dinner table. Every member of the family tries to be home for this important occasion. When all is ready, the father offers a prayer. Then the meal begins, including *mazoth* (unleavened bread), bitter herbs, parsley, lamb, and a mixture of chopped apples, nuts, cinnamon and wine. This meal is special because each of these foods reminds the Jewish people of some event, sweet or bitter, in the deliverance of their fathers from slavery many years ago. The Jew is one who remembers—the bondage in Egypt and the exodus through the Red Sea waters.

A Christian is one who remembers too. The Christian remembers the death and the resurrection of Christ. This remembering is at the heart of the two ordinances: baptism and the Lord's Supper.

The early church regarded baptism as the great act which once-for-all incorporates and embraces us into Christ. The Lord's Supper was then viewed as a continuing communion within that fellowship (Acts 2:41-47).

Like the Passover meal, the Lord's Supper uses eating and drinking as a way of remembering. We may be seated around a

146

We may be seated around a table and break bread. . . .

table and break bread from one loaf and drink from one cup. Or we may be seated in the pews and be served little pieces of bread, and wine (or grape juice) in small cups. This food becomes a visible reminder of Christ's broken body and His shed blood.

But why this meal? Why eat and drink? What more than remembrance does it mean?

OBSERVING THE LORD'S SUPPER

For nearly two thousand years Christians have found the Lord's Supper a necessary and helpful act of worship. Examine several accounts:

1. Begin by reading the oldest account of how the Lord's Supper was begun. Read 1 Corinthians 11:23-34. Try to answer these questions:
   a. When did Jesus institute the ordinance?
   b. What meanings did Jesus give to this act?
   c. What kind of preparation is necessary?
   d. What does the Lord's Supper say to life in the church? (See 1 Corinthians 11:17-22 here also.)

147

2. About 100 years later (A.D. 150) a Christian writer, Justin Martyr, wrote about the Lord's Supper in his day.

"And on the day which is called Sunday, there is an assembly in the same place of all who live in cities, or in country districts; and the records of the Apostles, or the writings of the prophets, are read as long as we have time. Then the reader concludes: and the president verbally instructs, and exhorts us, to the imitation of these excellent things: then we all together rise and offer up our prayers; and, as I said before, when we have concluded our prayer, bread is brought, and wine, and water; and the president, in like manner, offers up prayers, and thanksgivings, with all his strength; and the people give their assent by saying Amen: and there is a distribution, and a partaking by everyone, of the Eucharistic elements; and to those who are not present they are sent by the hands of the deacons."[35]

3. Here is a description of the Lord's Supper as observed by Anabaptists of the sixteenth century.

"When the Lord's Supper was distributed the minister took the bread and broke a piece of it for each, and as soon as it was given out and each had a piece in his hand, the minister also took a piece for himself, put it into his mouth and ate it; and immediately, seeing this, the congregation did the same. The minister, however, used no words, no ceremonies, and no blessing. As soon as the bread was eaten, the minister took a bottle of wine or a cup, drank, and gave each of the members of it."[36]

More important than the form, however, were the meanings of this act. An old parable from the early church was often used by the Anabaptists. Andreas Ehrenpreis writes in 1652:

"As the grain-kernels are together merged and each must give its content or strength into the one flour and bread, likewise also the wine, where the grapes are crushed under the press, and each grape gives away all its juice and all its strength into one wine. Whichever kernel and whichever grape, however, is not crushed and retains its strength for itself alone, such an one is unworthy and is cast out. This is what Christ wanted to bring home to His companions and guests at the Last Supper as an example of how they should be together in such a fellowship."[37]

WHAT DOES IT MEAN?

The early Christians probably observed the Lord's Supper at

every meeting for worship. At first it was a way of remembering the death of Christ, and sharing with each other their faith in His resurrection. An early word for this service was Eucharist, meaning thanksgiving.

In the centuries that followed, like baptism, the Lord's Supper took on the mysterious meanings of sacrament. The bread and wine, as reminders of Christ's broken body and blood poured out, emphasized the sacrifice. In the Mass conducted by the Roman Catholic Church, people came to believe that the bread and wine actually become the flesh and blood of Christ again. Attendance at Mass came to be seen as necessary for the forgiveness of sins. Many regarded the Mass as having an automatic benefit.

But as the case in baptism, our forefathers felt that the spirit and the attitude we bring to the Lord's Supper will largely determine the meaning it will have for us. As the bread is broken, we remember His broken body. As we drink from the cup, we remember His blood which was shed. It was love which led Him to the cross, and in this act He revealed God's love for us. When we take the bread and wine into our bodies, it is a symbol that we take also His spirit into our souls. If we take the bread and wine and not the loving spirit, we have missed the meaning of the communion service.

What then are the meanings the Lord's Supper may have for us? It can be:

1. *An act of remembrance.* We forget so easily. We need to remember the atoning death of Christ and that it was for us. We need also to keep alive the faith that Christ was victorious over sin and death. *"Do this in remembrance of me"* (1 Cor. 11:24).

2. *An act of renewal.* Here is a symbol which represents the constant renewal of our surrender to Christ and the renewal of His work in us. *"The cup of blessing . . . is it not a participation in the blood of Christ? The bread which we break, is it not a participation in the body of Christ?"* (1 Cor. 10:16).

3. *An act of fellowship with other Christians.* Here we remind

ourselves that we are not alone. We are members one of another! We participate in life with others. We are responsible for others. How intensely the early Christians believed in responsible community living is described in Acts 2:44-47. Many churches still receive an offering at the Lord's Supper to assist members within the brotherhood who have special needs.

4. *An act of hope.* In the Lord's Supper we look back to Christ's death and resurrection. We affirm the present reality of Christ and His church. And we look forward believing that whatever may come, Christ will be there. We *proclaim the Lord's death until he comes"* (1 Cor. 11:26). *Our Lord, come!* (1 Cor. 16:22).

PREPARING FOR COMMUNION

Since we believe the Lord's Supper has meaning only as we come to it in a right spirit, how do we prepare ourselves for it?

Paul, writing to the Corinthian Christians warned about taking the Lord's Supper *in an unworthy manner.* He asked that *a man examine himself* (1 Cor. 11:27-29).

Sometimes people stay away from communion because they feel they are not good enough. But no one really can be worthy in the sense of being good enough. Verse 29 suggests that the trouble lies in not *discerning the body.* When a spirit of reverence is lacking, when people fail to recognize the significance of this act of worship, or go through the motions while at odds with their fellow members in Christ's church, then the Lord's Supper is taken *unworthily.* This means that the person who is a sinner and knows it to be so, is perhaps better prepared to receive the Lord's Supper than the one who never sees his pride. The Lord's Supper must be approached in a spirit of humility.

In the past, many churches had a communion preparation service. Members were urged to straighten things out if they were not in harmony with the standards of the church. Sometimes, if there was division, a congregation would delay the communion service until broken relationships would be reconciled.

150

The practice of *foot washing,* based on John 13:1-17, has also been a part of the preparation for communion in some churches. Though few still continue the practice, the act emphasized humility and the willingness to be servant to others.

The congregations that place emphasis upon preparation for communion emphasize that the church is a disciplined body of believers. We are a people responsible to each other through our commitment to Christ. The Lord's Supper then has the greater meaning for us when we can participate in the knowledge of integrity, unity, and peace among the members. So some churches practice *closed communion.* Only the members of that particular local congregation who have taken binding vows for each other participate.

At the same time, other congregations remind us that the church dare never become exclusive. The church is an inclusive fellowship. It is for sinners as well as saints. In the Lord's Supper we express our fellowship in Christ, with all Christians—not only those who belong to Salem or Faith or First Church.

The words of invitation, spoken by the minister express this idea.

"This table of the Lord is open to all fellow Christians; and although none should partake of these sacred emblems impenitent or without faith in Christ, we cordially invite all who are sincerely seeking Him to come to His table, in the assurance that He who came into the world to be the Savior of all will in no wise cast them out.

Come to this table, not because you must, but because
you may;
come to testify not that you are righteous, but that
you sincerely love our Lord Jesus Christ, and
desire to be His true disciples;
come, not because you are strong, but because you are
weak; not because you have any claim in heaven's
mercy and help;
come, not to express an opinion, but to seek a Presence
and pray for a Spirit."[38]

151

WORDS TO REMEMBER

Communion. Full spiritual relationships between persons; participation in the ordinance of the Lord's Supper.

Mass. In the Roman Catholic Church, the celebration of the Lord's Supper, which emphasizes the sacrifice of Christ in each observance of the Mass.

Eucharist. An early term for the Lord's Supper, meaning "thanksgiving."

The Bread, the Cup. The elements (a loaf or small pieces of bread, wine or grape juice) used in the Lord's Supper.

TO LEARN MORE ABOUT COMMUNION

1. Read the articles "communion" and "Lord's Supper" in the *Mennonite Encyclopedia* for a more complete description of the observance of the Lord's Supper in the Mennonite church.

2. Often our own faith becomes more meaningful when we try to understand the beliefs and practices of other Christians. Do you have friends who belong to the Roman Catholic Church, or the Christian or Disciples of Christ denomination, or the Church of the Brethren? You may want to attend one of these churches with a friend to find out: How is the Roman Catholic Mass observed? What recent changes have been made in the Mass? Why does the Christian Church observe communion every Sunday? What is the Church of the Brethren's "love feast" like?

3. John 15:1-17, "I am the vine, you are the branches . . ." is often read at the communion service. Why is this an appropriate passage for the Lord's Supper? What does it say about our relationship to Christ, and to fellow members in the church?

35. Anne Fremantle, editor, *A Treasury of Early Christianity* (New York: The Viking Press, 1953), p. 341.

36. *Mennonite Encyclopedia,* Vol. I (Scottdale: Herald Press, 1955), p. 652.

37. *Mennonite Encyclopedia,* Vol. III (Scottdale: Herald Press, 1957), p. 394.

38. Charles Wallis, ed., *The Table of the Lord* (New York: Harper and Brothers, 1958), p. 3.

Chapter 20

The Mission of the Church

"Go therefore and make disciples of all nations, baptizing them in the name of the Father and of the Son, and of the Holy Spirit, teaching them to observe all that I have commanded you; and lo, I am with you always, to the close of the age." Matthew 28:19, 20.

WHAT'S THE CHURCH FOR ANYWAY?

How do you like this description of a successful church?

"The Choir's Fun Night Wednesday, August 30, brings a delightful summer of church activities to a climax. This will have been the busiest summer thus far our church has had. Beach parties, workdays, car washes, potlucks, fun nights, outings at the Bowl, theater, and ball park have added up to enriching the lives of hundreds."

Among the serious criticisms leveled at the church is this: that the ministry of Christ has been perverted into a social hour. Organization has taken the place of love, and ideas have taken the place of deeds.

Peter Marshall once said: "Many Chrisitans are like deep-sea divers dressed in suits designed for fathoms deep, marching bravely to pull stoppers from bathtubs." And Samuel Shoemaker declares: "We must repent of gambling for such small stakes when the church is out to save the world."

Why really is the church? Why does the church exist?

153

THE CHURCH'S MISSION—BECOMING SERVANT

When we ask, "What does the church do?" we come back to Jesus Christ. For the picture of what the church is to be and to do is found in the life, ministry, death, and resurrection of Jesus Christ. Jesus came among men as a servant. His mission, and ours through the church, is described by words like these:

"I have other sheep, that are not of this fold;

I must bring them also, and they will heed my voice" (Jn. 10:16).

"As thou didst send me into the world, so I have sent them into the world" (Jn. 17:18).

"You shall receive power when the Holy Spirit has come upon you; and you shall be my witnesses . . ." (Acts 1:8).

The Letter to the Ephesians is a letter about the church. God's plan, according to this letter, includes:

1. Sending Christ *to unite all things in him . . .* (1:10).
2. Making Christ head of the church, *which is his body . . .* (1:23).
3. Making known *through the church the manifold wisdom of God* (3:10).
4. Supplying the church with the gifts that equip the people of God for this ministry (4:11, 12).

Through the church we participate in the continuing work of God in today's world. As Jesus' ministry was that of being servant, so the church's mission is not to itself alone, but service to the world as well. Archbishop William Temple spoke of the church as the only society in the world which exists for those who are not members of it!

"God whom the church is called to serve is the God of the world. He created it, loves it, works in it . . . He aims to heal the world and give it unity . . . Christians are called to participate in the mission and reconciliation of the universe . . . The church does not exist for itself; it exists for the world."[39]

THE LOCAL MISSION OF THE CHURCH

We begin where we are. For most of us the church means First or Bethel or Grace Church. We cannot easily think of

154

church without thinking of a building or a congregation meeting for worship each Sunday. And our commitment to Christ includes identifying ourselves with God's people at a particular time and place.

What is our mission in the congregation? For most of us it includes providing and supporting:

A church building as a place of worship, study, and fellowship. The building can also stand in the community as a symbol of faith, as a witness to Jesus Christ, if the congregation is faithful.
A pastor to proclaim and interpret God's word, to assist people in recognizing God at work, and to help the church discover its mission.
The responsibility for nurture and growth—Sunday school, Bible study, discussion, research and action groups. . . .
Local mutual aid—material help and encouragement to people in need, emergency, disaster.

At what points do you already participate in the local mission of the church?

In what other ways can you begin to serve?

THE LARGER MISSION OF THE CHURCH

In thinking about mission, many Christians have a peculiar temptation. When we come to church every Sunday, and go to

The larger mission of the church.

Sunday school, give a tithe (or at least a couple of coins each week), sing in the choir, serve as ushers, and serve on a committee or two, we may begin to feel that we are awfully busy in the church, and that we are doing our mission.

But we dare not think of church membership simply in terms of what we do *within* the organization of the church. There is nothing more useless than a church program that focuses only upon the church members. The purpose of the church is to make Christ Lord and Master of every life. And the purpose of the church gathered on Sundays is that God's people may be engaged in mission not only an hour or two on Sunday morning, but throughout the week.

Loren Halverson, in *Exodus into the World,* writes, "The world is not impressed or interested in what goes on within the tent. The world neither hears nor understands what is said there. Our gestures of piety (no matter how sincere) as we go through the activities of the tent are not noticed. But what we say, do, and are in the midst of man within the context, language, and problems of life is noticed very well."[40]

At one time the church building was the center of community life. But no longer is this true in many areas. People may live in one community and work in another. Today the church needs to reckon with facts like

> Specialization in work, automation
> Different working hours
> The long weekend, leisure and recreation
> Travel and movement of people
> Growing cities
> Wealth and poverty
> Centralized decision-making and power blocks in city, government, labor, management
> Many people will never enter the church.

The church of today needs mission outposts—not only in India, Congo, and Brazil, but in Kansas, Pennsylvania, California, and Ontario—wherever the people are. The outpost may be a home in the suburbs, a teen recreation center, or an inner-city day nursery. Or it may capitalize on work relationships—the car pool and lunch pail circle. High schools and the university campuses become places for the Christian witness.

Today's changing communities may call for bold experiments to go where the people are.

The Quiet Place, a little coffee shop and bookstore on Chicago's South Side, is staffed by members of the Woodlawn Mennonite Church. Begun as a way to get in touch with the people of the community, this mission outpost of one congregation is described by Marie J. Regier. "We find many times when we can say 'yes, this store is sponsored by the church.' And to people's questions we can answer with what our church believes. We know there are some who have come into our church through the contact at the Quiet Place. But we are not just out to get members. If persons can feel the breath of God in the Quiet Place, we are satisfied."

"By the time you are grown up, the form of the church will have changed beyond recognition," said D. Bonhoeffer to a youth at his baptism. The form of the church is continuing to change. The church in mission is outward-directed.

THE MANY-SIDED MISSION

God so loved the world. Because God loved the world He sent Jesus. Because He continues to love the world He sends the church of Christ into the world. God acts so that which has become divided, broken, and diseased . . . may be once more united, reconciled, and healed.

1. We bring our offerings, a part of our earnings, for the church's mission:

What does this many-sided mission include?

It provides ministers and teachers for churches and schools in many lands.

It prepares and distributes Christian literature that can speak to men about how God's love can help them in their lostness.

It sends doctors and nurses and medical supplies to bring

157

healing and hope where otherwise there would be suffering, pain, and premature death.

2. We send young people and older people, too, into places where acts of voluntary service can meet some human need.

3. We share our crops and clothing and blankets through the Mennonite Central Committee to bring help and hope to refugees from war or other disaster.

4. We build and staff church colleges and a seminary, and provide Sunday school materials for children and adults so that we may learn truth about ourselves, the world, and God at work, and how God would use us for His purposes.

5. We establish hospitals and mental hospitals and homes for the aged to serve the needs of the sick and aging.

6. When disaster strikes we lend a helping hand, a sympathetic ear, an encouraging word.

7. Challenging the idolatries of our culture, such as militarism and racism, we try to bring a voice of conscience and a positive witness of love.

A many-sided mission—but the purpose, the focus of this mission is to make Christ known as *Lord* and *Master* of every life!

THE TEAM APPROACH

God's mission demands a team approach. It is larger than any one man, or any one church, can handle alone. Jesus knew that He would never be able to reach all men personally. So He began by calling and engaging helpers. He called Simon and Andrew, James and John, and others to come and help.

God's mission through the church is not the minister's job alone. The minister's task is to help the church become the ministering (serving) church. Every Christian believer is needed for the mission.

Baptism affirms that one is united with Christ and His church, with God and His mission. There are no spectator Christians who pay at the gate, then sit and watch. We're all on the team, and there are no free passes.

But even this team, the congregation, is not enough. We join hands with other congregations in a conference of churches. The General Conference is made up of about 300 congregations, 55,000 members.

Beyond this, we are part of a larger team. We join hands with other Mennonite groups in support of Mennonite Central Committee, for example. We join hands with other denominations for certain kinds of witness. Perhaps it is a local church association or a city council of churches. It may be with a state council of churches for teacher training or witness to legislature. There are also national and worldwide associations such as NAE (National Association of Evangelicals), NCC (National Council of Churches), and WCC (World Council of Churches).

The days are past when one church or group of churches dares think it has a corner on the truth. The divisions of yesterday are a luxury the church can no longer afford. Instead of working against other Christians, or wastefully duplicating the efforts of others, we must continue the unique witness we can bring to the world. But we need also to join with other Christians in our common task, that of making Christ known as Lord and Master of every life.

WORDS TO REMEMBER

Mission. The task God has entrusted to the church. A mission is not something you *do*. It is something you *have*.

Ministry. The church's servant task. The minister is only a servant of God's people to help them become God's ministering people.

Witnessing. ". . . one beggar telling another beggar where to find bread." —D. T. Niles

HOW DO YOU SEE THE MISSION OF THE CHURCH TODAY?

1. Write a short statement about your understanding of the church's mission.

2. How is your congregation organized for ministry
   a) when the church is gathered?
   b) beyond the "home base"?
3. What do you find exciting about your church?
4. What would you criticize about your church?
5. Are there mission outposts in your community or area that your youth group could visit? What needs exist in your community that your church, perhaps your youth group, needs to consider as part of your ministry for Christ? The guide book, *Start Where You Are* by Walter Paetkau will be helpful here.[41]

A PRAYER AS YOU BEGIN
"Revive Thy Church, O Lord, beginning with me."

—Samuel Shoemaker

39. Colin W. Williams, *For the World* (New York: Council Press, 1965).
40. Loren E. Halverson, *Exodus into the World* (Minneapolis: Augsburg Publishing Company, 1966), p. 43.
41. Walter Paetkau, *Start Where You Are* (Newton, Kansas: Faith and Life Press, 1965).

Chapter 21

Living the Christian Life

A disciple is not above his teacher, but every one when he is fully taught will be like his teacher. Luke 6:40.
I therefore . . . beg you to lead a life worthy of the calling to which you have been called. . . . Ephesians 4:1

THE LOVE OF CHRIST LEAVES US NO CHOICE!

When tornadoes swept through the Upper Midwest States on Palm Sunday, 1965, 271 persons were killed and $200 million in property damage was suffered. For the next four and a half months, corps of volunteers moved through Indiana, Michigan, and Ohio "just helping out."

One of the largest organized efforts was that of Mennonite Disaster Service (MDS). Thousands of man days were given to cleaning up debris, repairing and building houses and barns.

Amos Zook, who had come from Pennsylvania to help, explained, "As Christians, we have to show love to our fellowmen."

Another worker added, "As Mennonites we believe in faith that acts, love that reaches out a helping hand. When the cows break through the fence, or the neighbor's barn catches fire, we say, 'Don't just stand there—do something!' "

Why does a man give his time, labor, and money to help others? A Kansas carpenter replied:

"My parents came from Russia in 1907. All our lives we've heard about the persecution of the Mennonites and how they went from one country to another until they finally settled here.

161

We want to help.

"That's why many of our boys are conscientious objectors, because our people have had such a history of wars and disasters. My folks appreciated a kind word from anybody because it was something they never heard in Russia.

"Because of the disasters our people have faced we can feel for other people when something happens, and we want to help. That's all there is to it. We want to help."

Mennonite Disaster Service, born at a Sunday school class picnic at Hesston, Kansas, in 1950, is one expression of *Christian Discipleship*. Underlying this and the many ways of showing Christian concern for others is the belief that "the love of Christ leaves us no choice!" (2 Cor. 5:14 NEB).

Discipleship has to do with responsible living. A person's actions must square with his Christian experience. A person's actions are the expression of his response to Christ. Discipleship involves seeing life in terms of living for others.

In this unit we think through the idea of being Christian in all our relationships. The next three sessions focus on our search for the Christian way in our relationships to other persons in government, in the home, and at work.

But where do we get the idea that every action, every relationship of our lives is affected by Christ's claim?

FOLLOWING CHRIST

In the Gospels, Jesus' ministry on earth begins with His bold call to men: "Follow me!" Peter, John, Matthew, and many others responded. They became disciples of Jesus.

Disciples were common in Jesus' day. The Jewish rabbis had disciples who were students of the law. The pupils of the Greek philosophers were called disciples. John the Baptist had disciples.

But Jesus was calling men to a different kind of discipleship. Jesus wanted more of men than merely their becoming learners of some religious truth. He wanted more than teachers of His teaching. He was calling men to commit themselves to Him, to accept His spirit and way of life. He asked men to accept Him personally as Savior and Lord.

This meant more than declaring that Christ rules over all people. It meant accepting the rule of Christ personally. The confession of the early Christians, "Jesus is Lord," meant a pledge of obedience. To give oneself, body and soul, to the person of the Lord, to share His life, His mission, His fate—this is the call to discipleship.

FOLLOWING REDISCOVERED

By the sixteenth century the Roman Catholic Church had come to emphasize the great importance of the sacraments for salvation. Holiness of life was seen as an impossibility except for a few of the people who lived in the monasteries and devoted their lifetime to prayers and acts of mercy. The Lutheran Reformation focused on man's sin and separation from God, and man's restoration by the grace of God. For Lutherans the essence of Christianity was the experience of forgiveness by faith.

But for the Anabaptists, along with faith was the concept of following. That is, the Anabaptists felt that an outward expression of the inner experience of forgiveness was essential to true faith. They felt that it was not enough to enjoy personal salvation. For them the key question was, "What does it mean to follow Christ?"

This question led them to the conclusion that one cannot come to God, except one come to Him together with one's brother.

Harold S. Bender, writing in *The Mennonite Encyclopedia,* describes this view of discipleship:

"The individual responds to the call of Christ, forsakes his life of sin and self, receives a new nature, comes under the lordship of Christ, and takes Christ's life and teachings as normative for himself and for the church, and indeed ultimately for the whole social order. . . .

"The uniqueness of Anabaptism lies in its conviction that Christ is more than a divine being to be worshiped, more than a Savior who brings forgiveness through the cross and deliverance from the penalty and power of sin; He is the Lord to be followed and obeyed, and with whom the Christian enters into a covenant that controls his whole life."[42]

THE KEY IS LOVE

In thinking about Christian behavior, we need to see the creative power of Christian love. Jesus commanded *"You shall love your neighbor as yourself"* (Mk. 12:31). Again He emphasized *that you love one another* (Jn. 13:34).

When Jesus or the New Testament writers talk about *love,* they refer to something else than love between a fellow and a girl. Our dreamy-toned "I love you" may simply mean "I love me, and want you." The Greek word for that kind of love is *eros.* Jesus didn't have erotic love in mind.

Nor is the New Testament *love* simply that feeling of relatedness we see between brothers or sisters of the same family. The Greek word for that is *philia.* Filial love, that which causes a family clan to stick together, is common among all kinds of people.

Not *eros,* not *philia.* Instead, the most frequently used word for love in the New Testament is *agape.* Agape refers to God's kind of love—love that does not depend upon love in return. This love is concern for those whom it is easy to like and for those difficult to appreciate. *Agape* is interested not primarily in self, but in others.

But who can do that? Who can love everybody? Only as we discover how God loves us, and through Jesus Christ redeems us, is it possible for us to *love* in this new creative way. Becoming a Christian involves our trusting in God and depending on Him to help us *love*. And instead of finding this restrictive, Christian love opens up an exciting new way of life!

AN EXAMPLE OF LOVE IN CONFLICT

In the early days of the Freedom Movement, the Negroes of Montgomery, Alabama, stopped riding the city buses as a protest to the indignities heaped on them through the system of segregation. Often a white man entering the bus would demand the

One cannot come to God, except one come to Him together with one's brother.

165

seat already occupied by a Negro woman. Or the Negroes were forced to stand at the back of the bus while there were still empty seats in front. And so they chose to walk.

A young Negro minister, Martin Luther King, became the leading spokesman for the Negroes in Montgomery. One night, while the Rev. King's wife and baby were home alone, his home was bombed. He rushed home to find a crowd gathered outside. They were in an angry mood, ready to answer violence with violence. King pleaded with them to go to their homes. "Please be peaceful. We believe in law and order . . . I want you to love our enemies. . . ."

Not all acts in Montgomery, or in the Freedom Movement, have been acts of Christian discipleship. But through Martin Luther King's guidance, many persons in this situation discovered a creative power in love. Love helped them see that anger and violence are often motivated by fear. When the Negro people did not strike back with violence after their homes and churches were bombed, the fear of the white community began to lessen. And some of the Negroes, who had previously felt only hate, began to feel pity for those who clung so desperately to the system of segregation. They now began to see the white man as a brother who needed help if he would be freed of the chains of prejudice and fear and anger. It remains to be seen whether the Freedom Movement can keep its early vision and avoid methods of violence.

THE DILEMMA OF DISCIPLESHIP

Looking back to the Anabaptist attempt to rediscover the genius of the early Christian church, Mennonites have emphasized the discipleship life. This has included:

1. Obedience to the Great Commission (Mt. 28:19, 20). The missionary task belongs to every Christian believer. This task is more important than our job.

2. Love and nonresistance. To reconcile the love of God with the hatred and violence of war has seemed utterly impossible. Though recognizing that restraints on evil are necessary (Rom. 13: 1-8), Mennonites have generally withdrawn from participation in

war or high public office, leaving this to others. The positive emphasis has been on building strong communities of love and brotherhood through personal relationships.

3. Suffering in the spirit of cross-bearing. This willingness to bear suffering without striking back cost the lives of many (about 10,000 Anabaptist martyrs by the year 1600). More recently the spirit of cross-bearing has motivated a large worldwide relief program (MCC), voluntary service (VS), and disaster service (MDS).

4. The separated life of holiness. Following Christ meant putting away "all the works of darkness," including vulgar conversation, pride, drunkenness, immorality. A high moral standard of life is the fruit of repentance and obedience to Christ.[43]

Anabaptism has stood for the kind of Christianity expressed in the life of the early church. But the church as a whole has rejected this concept of Christian discipleship. And later generations of Mennonites find this kind of following Christ difficult, and often too costly. Why?

Our dilemma is that of being Christians in a sinful world. How can Christian faith penetrate our secular world? How can Christianity speak to our human history without being choked by the many forces of our time which do not move on the level of the gospel?

WORDS TO REMEMBER

Disciple. Pupil; a follower of Christ.

Lordship. Recognizing the complete claim of Jesus Christ upon our lives, and His Spirit a present reality.

Sonship. Our relationship to God. Jesus has declared us acceptable to God, and an heir of His life.

Ethics. Our way of life including our motives and acts, and the rightness and wrongness of such behavior.

THE CRUCIAL IMPORTANCE OF LIVING AS A CHRISTIAN

1. Some of Paul's letters follow a simple outline:
   a) proclaiming God's work in Christ, and
   b) what this means for our lives.

Note Ephesians 4:1 and Colossians 3:1 as points where the focus shifts from doctrine to the application for life.

2. New Testament passages that have lists of relationships in which the Christian lives include: Romans 13, Colossians 3:8—4:1, and Ephesians 5:21—6:9. What are these major relationships? What guiding principle is listed here that can help us to be Christian?

3. In looking back over the sections on "Following Christ" and "The Dilemma of Discipleship," how do you feel about your own life as a follower of Christ? In what areas of your life do you feel more growth is needed?

42. *Mennonite Encyclopedia,* Vol. IV (Scottdale: Herald Press, 1959), p. 1076.

43. J. Lawrence Burkholder, "The Anabaptist Vision of Discipleship," in Guy F. Hershberger, ed., *Recovery of the Anabaptist Vision* (Scottdale: Herald Press, 1957), pp. 138ff.

Chapter 22

Being a Christian Citizen

Let every person be subject to the governing authorities. For there is no authority except from God, and those that exist have been instituted by God." Romans 13:1

They've been over this one before. Now the Air Force recruitment poster gets them going again:

Dennis: "Think I'll enlist this summer. Maybe I can get into the Strategic Air Command. Gene just got out—after four years. He's been all over the world."

Tim: "I don't see it that way. I'm not sure about the value of those SAC bombers in the air all the time. I think we're just pushing Russia and China to build more weapons. How would we feel if their planes flew all around us, ready to drop those bombs? Besides, how can we think of ever using H-bombs, or any other kind of bombs?"

Dave: "Aw, come on Tim, where else can you find the freedoms we have? How are we going to keep the communists from taking them away? We might as well face it, a strong army is the only thing other countries really respect. Maybe someday we'll live in peace without war, but not yet. Besides, if they need me I've got to do my duty. Somebody's got to do it."

Tim: "That's just it. I'd like to know—What is my duty? When a fellow shoots down another man on the street, it's murder. But in the jungles of Vietnam it's okay. If a bomb would drop on Chicago, it'd be a terrible disaster, but on some far-off city in Asia—who cares? Aren't those people God's people, too? Who can tell me that it's my duty to kill?"

169

WHAT IS GOVERNMENT?

Many forces affect our lives and determine our actions. Among the most powerful of these is government.

Government, the system of order by which a society operates, takes many forms. The simplest form is the family in which father and mother provide for and protect their children. In primitive societies this then broadened out into the tribe or clan. This is the kind of government we find among the early Hebrew people. In the stories of Abraham and Jacob in Genesis, we observe how the father or oldest son becomes head of the tribe.

In ancient Greece, government was centered in the leading cities so that powerful city-states, like Sparta and Athens, developed. The Greek idea of power residing in the citizens is behind our idea of democracy.

In Jesus' time the most powerful government was seated in Rome, in the person of the emperor. Caesar's will and word became law. The Roman conquest and occupation of nation after nation encircled the Mediterranean until thirty provinces were controlled by the emperor and governed by his appointed men.

Governments have ranged from one-man rule, in which the king (or dictator) may own the land and literally own the people, to democracies in which the people rule. The form with which we are most familiar is a representative democracy or republic. Persons elected or appointed by the people carry out the government functions.

Governments may emphasize individualism, "He who governs best governs least." Or they may be socialist in which much or most of the property is owned and controlled by the government.

In our day, nationalistic states assume tremendous powers. In the United States, for example, one of every nine persons is employed by the government. In 1966 the cost of the federal government was $120 billion, one-fifth of the national income. But before we assume that government is the big bad bully dominating our lives, let us list a few of the many ways government relates to our lives.

170

GOVERNMENT AND YOU

Every letter you receive, the roads on which you drive, the school you attend, and the money you use are functions of government. So, too, are licensing, taxing, the system of law courts, police and fire protection, seeding and selling quotas for farmers, social security, regulation of advertising and packaging, and hundreds of other activities that restrain or benefit us.

Some functions of government are carried out by people in your community such as the postman, schoolteacher, or jury member. Others originate in the State House or from Washington, D.C., or Ottawa.

But there is more than government simply affecting us in ways we may think good or evil. Election time reminds us that we are also involved in determining policies by the kind of government we choose.

So, what shall our attitude be?

HELP FROM THE BIBLE?

The New Testament does not speak about democracy or communism. Nor will we find out anything about the merits of Republicans or Democrats, Conservatives or Liberals. There is plenty about Sadducees, Zealots, and Romans to give us some clues about Christian attitudes toward those who are in authority. Consider these examples:

1. Jesus
   a. In His temptations Jesus rejected the use of political power to accomplish His purpose (Mt. 4:7-10).
   b. Jesus refused to follow the urging of His Zealot friends and followers to become a political Messiah (Jn. 6:15).
   c. Jesus, living under the Roman rule, maintained a critical attitude toward it, yet denounced every attempt to overthrow it (Mk. 12:16, 17; Mt. 26:52).

2. Paul
   a. Paul sees rulers as necessary to maintain order in this

present age, although their methods are not always those of God's children (Rom. 12:14—13:14; 1 Cor. 6:1-3).

  b. Paul used his Roman citizenship and the protection of the soldiers (Acts 16:35-39; 22:25ff.).

  c. Paul urges not only respect, but prayer and support for those in positions of public responsibility (1 Tim. 2:1, 2).

  d. Toward the end of Paul's life there may be reference to the increasing hostile power of the reigning Caesar when Paul speaks of being rescued "from the lion's mouth" (2 Tim. 4:17).

3. Peter
  a. Peter is clear about the Christian's first loyalty: *We must obey God rather than men* (Acts 5:29).

  b. Christian freedom must be used responsibly. As a servant of God, the Christian will also show respect for governing authorities (1 Pet. 2:13-17).

4. The Revelation of John

John, exiled on the isle of Patmos about A.D. 96, writes while Christians are being severely persecuted. The Roman Emperor Domitian was trying to force emperor worship on the Christians. Government can become "the beast" when it assumes the place of God (Rev. 13:1-4).

But note—John did not advocate revolt, as Jesus had not advocated violence to overthrow an evil government. The first century Christian refused to bow to government, when doing so would violate his first allegiance to God. Often this meant the way of suffering and death.

OUR MENNONITE HERITAGE

The Anabaptists of the sixteenth century accepted the role of government as God-ordained. They believed government necessary "to punish the evil, to protect the good, to administer a righteous justice, to care for the widows, the orphans and the poor, and to provide a police force that is not against God and His Word."[44]

The Christian is obedient. His response to authority that conflicts with God is not violent overthrow of government. But the Anabaptists refused to baptize children, refused to bear arms and to take the oath as protest by example.

For the Anabaptists believed Christ alone is Lord of conscience. And so they chose not to participate in government. Government rule means might and lordship. To be a Christian means to serve, even if this involves suffering, persecution, and death.

Office-holding was rejected in the belief that the church of Christ must be separate from the world. Later in Europe, and more recently in America, Mennonites have participated in government to the extent of holding office. The Mennonite Church (OM) and Amish continue to forbid participation in more than local government.

Bearing arms in war is contrary to the teaching and spirit of Christ (Mt. 5:38-45). During World War II over 4000 Mennonite fellows served in Civilian Public Service camps. From 1952-1966 over 10,000 Mennonite young men have spent two years in 1-W service as an alternative to military service.

Use of *the law courts* has been discouraged. Members of the Christian brotherhood should settle differences among themselves in the spirit of Christian love (1 Cor. 6:1-7). However, Mennonites have frequently seen a difference between use of attorney for defense, and being the aggressive party in a lawsuit. Also, in the complex economy of the twentieth century, there are many necessary legal proceedings such as clearance of title for real estate, settlement of estates, etc. Many of these do not necessarily involve conflict of personal relationships.

Swearing of oaths is wrong according to Matthew 5:34-37. The Christian shall speak truth at all times, not only when he has his hand on the Bible. Calling on God's name in this manner is abusive of the sacred name of deity. It is acceptable to affirm to the truth rather than to swear.

In summary, how has our church viewed relationships to the government?

1. The Christian is a law-abiding citizen, respecting the law and authority which is here for order.

2. The Christian will not use the tactics of violence and rebellion to change bad laws or influence government, but will witness by persuasion, and by personal suffering if necessary.

3. The Christian cannot bless all functions of government.

WHAT ABOUT WAR AND NONRESISTANCE?

"Our 'Skyraider' was loaded with 750- and 500-pound napalm bombs. . . . Our wing load carried 7,500 pounds of high explosive anti-personnel bombs. We were in the lead plane going in . . ." tells Bernard Fall, professor at Howard University, about his observation flight with an American attack group in Vietnam.

"As we flew over the target it looked to me very much as the normal village would look: on the edge of a river, sampans and fishnets in the water. It was a peaceful scene. Major Carson put our plane into a steep dive. I could see the napalm bombs dropping from the wings. The big bombs, first. As we peeled back from our dive, I saw an incredibly bright flash of fire as napalm exploded at tree level. The first pass had a one-two effect. The napalm was expected to force the people out into the open. Then the second plane was to move in with heavy fragmentation bombs to hit whoever had rushed out into the open. So our wingman followed us in and dropped his heavy explosives. Mushroom-like clouds drifted into the air.

"We made a second pass and dropped our remaining 500-pound bombs. Our wingman followed. Then we went in for a third time and raked over the village with our cannon. We came down low, flying very fast, and I could see some of the villagers trying to head away from the burning shore in their sampans. The village was burning fiercely. I will never forget the sight of the fishnets in flame, covered with burning, jellied gasoline. Behind me I could hear, even through my padded helmet, the roar of our plane's 20-millimeter cannon as we flew away.

I will never forget the sight of the fishnets in flame.

"There were probably between 1,000 and 1,500 people living in the fishing village we attacked. It is difficult to estimate how many were killed. It is equally difficult to judge if there actually were any Vietcong in the village, and if so, if any were killed. . . ."[45]

War is hell. War is a denial of Christ's purpose for people. Rooted in national pride, war makes things out of persons; it makes them instruments, or targets. But persons remain persons however we wish to consider them.

Christian nonresistance is based on Christ's command to love all men (Lk. 6:27, 28). This means more than rejection of war and simply choosing an alternative to military service. Christian nonresistance has a positive dimension—that of sacrificial service to men who are in need at all times and under all circumstances.

As members of a historic peace church (along with the Friends and Brethren), Mennonites have sometimes felt alone in this position. But the Christian church was pacifist for the first three hundred years after Christ. And today, following the tragedy of two world wars, and the growing possibilities of nuclear destruction, there is a new awareness that the church can no longer bless war. In our kind of world the role of the Christian as peacemaker and reconciler takes on new importance.

WORDS TO REMEMBER

Government. The system of order by which a society is organized and operates.

Pacifism. Refusal to participate in war, or to use violence as a form of social action.

Nonresistance. A form of pacifism growing out of the conviction that Christian love must become the positive concern which we as Christians have for others.

HOW WILL YOU SERVE GOD AND COUNTRY?

1. SSS Form 150 is the special form for conscientious objectors to war. Try your hand at two of the questions asked:
    a. Describe the nature of your belief which is the basis of your claim (for exemption from the Armed Forces) and state whether or not your belief in a Supreme Being involves duties which to you are superior to those arising from any human relation.
    b. Under what circumstances, if any, do you believe in the use of force?

2. How do you feel about this suggestion: "Why could not the Holy Spirit lead us to expect at least two years voluntary service from every believing young person . . . even if no Selective Service were prodding him or her? Why could not individual persons remaining at home pledge a year's support for such volunteers?"

3. Segregation of schools was finally declared illegal by the Supreme Court. What existing laws might be considered unjust?

What steps can the Christian take to change unjust laws or to witness to government? nonparticipation? migration to another country? letter-writing? personal or delegation visits to congressmen? boycott? public demonstration? prayer? Evaluate these and other possibilities.

44. *Mennonite Encyclopedia,* Vol. IV (Scottdale: Herald Press, 1959), p. 612.

45. *They Are Our Brothers,* Fellowship of Reconciliation pamphlet (Nyack, New York, 1966), pp. 7, 8.

Chapter 23

Being Christian in the Home

He answered, "Have you not read that he who made them from the beginning made them male and female, and said, 'For this reason a man shall leave his father and mother and be joined to his wife, and the two shall become one'? So they are no longer two but one. What therefore God has joined together, let no man put asunder. . . ." Then children were brought to him. . . . Jesus said, "Let the children come to me, and do not hinder them; for to such belongs the kingdom of heaven." Matthew 19:4-6, 13, 14

HOME IS MANY THINGS

Mother is on the phone making plans for a housewarming party for the new neighbors. Susan is about ready to blow her top because she is waiting for the phone. Ralph is singing at the top of his lungs in the bathroom, so that Mother has to cover one ear and ask her friend at the other end of the line to talk louder. Dad has resorted to a mirror in the kitchen to shave. The drone of the razor adds an eerie overtone to all the other noises.

Home can be a nightmare—sometimes—when, for example, Gayle storms out of the living room screaming, "Why do I always get picked on? Why me?" slams the door, flings herself on the bed, and sobs. Or when Jim sulks because Dad suddenly needs the car tonight after all. And after Jim had it all arranged to take Sharon, and Don and Becky to the game. Now they'll all have to ride the bus!

And worse than a nightmare when Marcene and Cal, married two years, sit at the dinner table, deliberately picking at the food. An icy wall of silence between them. Why is Cal gone more and more evenings? wonders Marcene. Why is Marcene no longer as excitingly beautiful as she once seemed? wonders Cal. Both are afraid to speak. But something has gone wrong. Every time they start to talk about it, they end up arguing. It can't go on this way. . . .

But home is also where we get our nearest taste of the experience of heaven. Home—where baby and toddler learn early the secure warmth of Mother and Daddy's love. Home—where the young teen knows deep down that Mom and Dad really do care. Home—where we can take off our shoes, and where sweatshirt and jeans and curlers are in. Home—where we can talk, and say what we

Home can be a nightmare.

really feel; where we discover what love and forgiveness is all about; where, in spite of our most glaring faults, we are still accepted and needed.

We live as part of a home now. Within three or five or ten years most of us will begin our own homes. What does it mean to be Christian as we think of marriage, or life in our home now?

GUIDANCE FROM THE BIBLE

Three Scripture passages that speak about relationships in the home are:

Ephesians 5:21—6:4
Colossians 3:18-21
1 Peter 3:1-7

1. What is the principle suggested that can make for harmonious relationships in the family?

2. What should be the wife's attitude toward her husband?

3. What is the husband's responsibility toward his wife?

4. What do you see here that is necessary for a healthy relationship between parents and their children?

5. Do you have any disagreements with the advice given in these passages? If so, on what points? Why?

PREPARING FOR MARRIAGE

Our society is made up of families. Almost every girl hopes someday to marry. Most every fellow wants to find a good girl who will become his wife.

As we get to be 13 or 14 or 15, we suddenly become aware of new powers and forces in us. Sometimes these forces and pulls frighten us a little. Girls who used to think boys were just horrid begin to discover they can attract fellows. More than that, they begin to enjoy the attention the fellows show. And these same fellows who used to detest having anything to do with girls begin to discover amazing delight in being with girls. At first this socializing with members of the opposite sex is done in the security of the group. Then begins the dating, steadies, engagement, and finally the climax of marriage.

Dating may be considered a hallway leading to marriage. It provides an opportunity for maturing teen-agers to learn to know each other more personally in many areas of thought, conduct, and activity.

Sometimes twisted ideas of dating prevail, when questions like these seem important. How far shall you go on a date? What about kissing? What about "going all the way"?

But love dare not be confused with physical attraction. Love is holy and sacred. Eric Fromm, the psychiatrist said about love: "To love somebody is not just a strong feeling—it is a decision, it is a judgment, it is a promise."

To love is to take full responsibility for the care of the one loved. Love is on an unsound foundation when it is based too largely on the physical expressions of it. Petting arouses urges that should not and cannot find proper and healthy expression outside of marriage.

The more casual relationships of dating can help us cultivate friendship with members of the opposite sex. There is value in learning to know many fellows and girls. For early teens, group get-togethers are preferred rather than pairing off too quickly. Going steady among high schoolers tends to cut off the opportunity of knowing others and to tempt risky intimacies.

Engagement is that announcement, after a time of courting, when two people declare they have found each other. Engagement is more than giving or receiving a diamond, however. This is the time when a couple makes specific plans for marriage and life together. Now the two need to think together and talk seriously about where they will live, their work, their attitudes toward money, children, and the church. Though they don't "marry the family," they will be sensitive to the feelings of their parents and learn to know the "in-laws-to-be."

This is an important time to begin praying together. And prayer should be easy—in that sense of excitement and joy in which we can thank God for the privilege of sharing our life with this wonderful person. The period of engagement is also a time to listen and to share misgivings and fears with a trusted counselor.

How long should engagement be? No rule fits every situation. But perhaps three months to one year is an optimum time for most couples.

A Christian wedding will give serious consideration to concerns as:

1. The church's involvement. Can a Christian wedding really be a private affair? Marriage is one of those great events that needs to be shared with the Christian fellowship. It may not be practically possible to invite the congregation to the wedding. At least the wedding should be announced in advance so that the congregation can pray for the couple.

2. Worship service rather than show. Plan for your wedding early, but not simply on the basis of what you have seen at other weddings. Plan with your pastor to make it a service of praise to God and a time of prayer for God's blessing upon the home you are beginning. Flowers, candles, photographer, clothes, and wedding party ought not to overshadow the spirit of the occasion. The music is important. For a worship service, the great hymns of the church contribute far more than traditional wedding marches and some of the other sentimental tunes and lyrics that have found their way into the church.

3. Vows made to God. The marriage form has this or a similar question to which groom and bride are asked to respond: "Do you in the presence of God and these witnesses take———— to be your wedded wife (husband), to love and cherish, to comfort and sustain her (him), in health or sickness, in prosperity or adversity, to live with her (him) in peace as becometh a faithful Christian

husband (wife), exercising patience, forbearance, kindness; and, forsaking all others, keep yourself to her (him), and her (him) alone, as long as you both shall live?" The "I do" is more than a simple legal contract. It is a vow to God as well. How then can these vows in the wedding service have their full and deepest meanings if either the groom or the bride is not a committed Christian? An interfaith marriage needs to be given far more serious thought than is frequently done.

4. Let all plans contribute to the happy but holy and serious purpose of marriage, including the kind of reception you plan, and the wedding trip.

BUILDING A CHRISTIAN HOME

When the minister says, "I now pronounce you husband and wife," and the wedding is over, the real task has just begun—building a Christian home. Marriage is not "one big Saturday night." It is for keeps.

The first days are high with the excitement of giving oneself completely to another person. Being on your own, setting up housekeeping, doing things together, are grand! But the emotional excitement wears off. Decisions have to be made. Bills must be paid. And believe it or not, that other person is not completely perfect! Many adjustments have to be made by both partners in a marriage.

"Let there be spaces in your togetherness," wrote Kahlil Gibran in *The Prophet*. If two persons are to complement each other, they must do more than focus upon themselves. They must cultivate

Often the birth of a baby helps a young couple.

the friendship of others, develop hobbies and interests, and find a worthy purpose for their life together.

Often the birth of a baby helps a young couple deepen their relationship of trust and dependence. This little helpless child, the fruit of their love for each other, God's gift to them, needs them. And as the child grows and looks to them, they discover that parenthood involves more than bringing a child into the world. Parenthood is more than providing food and clothing. It also demands the giving of a faith. And often parents discover that they still need to become that which they thought they already were.

WHEN MARRIAGE FAILS—DIVORCE

Getting married is not difficult. Millions of couples marry every year. Most of them believe that their marriage will be happy. They want their marriage to work. But about one of every four marriages in this country ends in divorce.

To speak of divorce, the legal ending of a marriage, is to recognize marriage as a legal contract. For the person who views marriage as no more than a contract of convenience, divorce may raise no particular "right or wrong" questions. But for the Christian, it is different.

Yet it happens. What if a couple simply cannot build a happy marriage? What if it doesn't work? Isn't divorce sometimes better all around than staying married? Can a divorced person marry again?

These are tough questions for the Christian. Important Scripture passages that reflect Jesus' attitude regarding divorce include: Mark 10:2-13; Matthew 5:31, 32 and 19:1-12; and 1 Corinthians 7:10, 11.

Jesus makes it plain that God's purpose is a stable family life, and that divorce is no part of that purpose. The Christian cannot enter marriage with the back door open, "We can always get out of it if it doesn't work."

For divorce is never a happy solution. Always it is an admission of failure. Usually also it is an admission of unwillingness to make the sacrifices necessary to build a meaningful marriage relationship.

But what of the person who is divorced, or who remarries after divorce? Certainly we believe God can forgive human sin. And the church needs to surround such unfortunate persons with love and understanding rather than bitter judgment. But always the hurt and scars of such an experience remain.

The prevalence of divorce does say to us that Christians must take the meaning of marriage far more seriously. Marriage is for mature persons. As one fellow, married at eighteen and divorced at twenty-one, said: "Marriage is easy to get into, and it's fun for awhile; but it's awfully hard to get out of, and it hurts when you do it."

Love, at its richest, can be known only by those who forego a low order of love in order to experience honest joy. Plan for a marriage that will last fifty years and get ready for it. Shortcuts in something so important are paid for dearly.

ON MANAGING OUR PARENTS

"Difficulties with parents are often the reflections of difficulties within ourselves. Because we feel insecure, or guilty, or sorry for ourselves . . . we give vent to our feelings. About the only people we can talk to freely are Mother and Dad, so . . . they get the brunt of the storm. . . .

"Take Mother and Dad into your confidence. Put as much effort into being friends with your folks as you do into your friendships at school. Remember, parents are human. They'll respond to kindness."[46]

The basic rule of the Minnesota Teen-age Code, developed jointly by youth and adults under the sponsorship of the Governor's Youth Council is: "Parents should know where their sons and daughters are while away from home, what they are doing, and with whom they are spending their time. Parents should also know what time their young people return home." Why are these things important?

HOW WILL YOU MAKE YOUR FAMILY RELATIONSHIPS CHRISTIAN?

1. What irks you about your parents? Now, what is there about yourself that must at times worry your parents? Be honest now! Since we cannot usually change someone else, what changes can you make that can help the situation? Where will you begin?

2. How do you feel about your relationship to other fellows and girls? Why do you feel others like to be with you, or try to avoid you? What is there about your experiences in dating that you are happy for, or regret?

3. What will you look for (qualities of character) in the fellow or girl you will want to marry? What advice should be given the girl who plans to marry a fellow to reform him?

4. Some families seem to have a lot of enjoyment in being together. Others are forever squabbling and are brought together only by funerals. What do you think makes the difference?

46. Robert A. Cook, *It's Tough to Be a Teen-ager* (Grand Rapids: Zondervan, 1955), pp. 34, 38.

Chapter 24

Being Christian in My Work

Whatever your task, work heartily, as serving the Lord and not men. . . ." Colossians 3:23

It was a beautiful day in a big, busy, dirty city. Two street cleaners, one on each side of the street moved slowly along, brushing the dirt into piles along the gutters. One was doing his job well, the other wasn't. At the corner, a man who had been watching, commented on the neat job. The cleaner looked up in surprise. Looking back over his work, he said in broken English, "She do looka good, huh?" Then, he pointed to the blue sky overhead and said, "God's world, she very beautiful. Me, I gotta go to work." With that he went on down the street sweeping into neat piles the refuse of a careless city.

Reuel Howe, observing the scene, comments: "There went a man with a menial job but a powerful sense of vocation, and the menial job had somehow become the means by which he pursued his vocation. . . . A job, any job that serves a constructive purpose, even a menial job, has the meaning of a ministry; and by our faithfulness to it, we serve both God and man."[47]

BUT I DON'T WANT TO BE A STREET CLEANER

Street cleaners are out anyway. Each night a man in neatly pressed uniform, in an air-conditioned, carpeted, electronics control room glances over the many buttons that line the walls. He selects one. The touch of a button . . . and whoosh! The streets are clean. At least somebody'll come up with a machine!

A whole set of new words is being coined to describe today's world of work. Words like automation . . . cybernetics . . . organization man . . . technopolis . . . leisure . . . guaranteed annual income. . . .

Fantastic changes in our job world have taken place in the last generation. A striking example is the farm. A hundred years ago, when there were only about 32 million people in the United States, about 65 percent of them lived on farms. American farm units reached an all-time peak in 1935 with 6.8 million. By 1961 there were only 3.7 million farms. By 1980 there may be less than 1.4 million farms. By then probably less than 5 percent of the country's 185 million people will live and work on the soil.[48]

The forces that have changed farming affect other employment too, Technology—machines replacing men. The science labs—opening up new fields of work, and making others obsolete—the assembly line, and giant corporations are changing our way of life. The rise of sprawling cities, megalopolises, stretching from Portland to Norfolk, along the Gulf Coast, or Southern California tell us that ours is an urban culture.

Today, of all people gainfully employed, 85 percent work for others. Service industries have expanded, while the number of workers engaged in producing goods has shrunk. Workdays and weeks become shorter; holidays and vacations become longer.

And even now, the effects of automation and cybernetics (hitching the computer to the machine) only begin to dawn on us. There will be fewer jobs. These will demand a higher level of skills. A man may need to train and retrain three or four times during his lifetime. Unemployed leisure will be forced upon larger numbers of people.

The furniture-maker of a former day could build a table from start to finish. Much of his satisfaction derived from the finished product. Part of his life was in that table. Today, in an assembly-line, wage-economy, the paycheck, at least, represents to a man the investment of his working time. What will happen when even this may be denied to many? when there are not enough jobs to go around? And what will happen when, for the first time, it may be possible to produce enough goods and services so that no person will need to live in poverty? What is the meaning of work and leisure in such a world?

THE CHRISTIAN'S VOCATION

Vocation, as *we* use it, usually means the profession or trade by which we earn a living. But in the New Testament, the word *vocation* means something other than a man's job. The word *vocation* is used only in Ephesians 4:1 (in the King James Version). The more common word is "calling." The New Testament uses the term to refer to God's call to repentance and faith, and to the life of fellowship and service in the church.

To be a Christian is our primary vocation, regardless of how we may earn our daily living. The Bible does not really speak of a man's being called to an earthly profession or trade. Paul, for example, is called by God to be an apostle. Although he was a tentmaker, he was not called to be one.

And so, vocation, in the biblical sense, is not first of all about a job. It is about finding God's will for our lives. A sense of vocation makes us ask, What is God's will for my life? How can my life fulfill the vocation of being a Christian? What is God's place for me in terms of the gifts He has given me?

To begin at this point is not to take lightly our daily work. It is precisely because the Christian is called of God that our work, our job, takes on significance. God is as concerned about what happens between Sundays as about what happens on Sunday morning. Christ, as Lord of life, means that Christ's claim upon life is a total claim. And a man's working time is one of the largest chunks of his life he has to give.

THE DIGNITY OF WORK

Throughout much of history, work has been looked upon as a hateful necessity. To the ancient Greeks, work was something to be left to slaves. The nobleman of old China could be identified by his long fingernails—to prove to the world that his hands were not sullied with toil.

Many people have viewed labor as a punishment for sin. This idea is rooted in the Genesis story of the expulsion of Adam and Eve from the Garden, and God's words to them: *In the sweat of your face you shall eat bread till you return to the ground* (Gen. 3:17-19).

But look at the creation story again. At the very beginning, man is created *to fill the earth and subdue it; and have dominion . . . over every living thing* (Gen. 1:28). He is placed in the garden *to till it and keep it* (Gen. 2:15). Work is the normal, natural, and healthy routine of human living.

The ancient command in Exodus 20:8-11 speaks not only of the need for rest, but the need also for the days of work. From the biblical point of view, work is neither a curse nor punishment, but an integral part of God's original intention in the creation of the world.

But what Genesis 3 tells us so forcefully is that *man is a rebellious creature*. And the consequence of human sin reaches into every area of human life, including our work. Man's work should be the sphere of our glad cooperation, with the Creator. It has now become the scene of bitter rivalry and quarreling. How often has that scene described in Genesis 4 (Cain and Abel) been repeated? Paul writes to Timothy in language we can understand: *The love of money is the root of all evils . . .* (1 Tim. 6:10).

Work is not a curse. But it is man's rebellion against God that turns even a man's work into a thing of bitterness—the ground is full of *thorns and thistles* (Gen. 3:18).

But the Bible's message is redemption. Jesus of Nazareth, supreme instrument of God's redemption, was a worker with His hands, a carpenter. When Jesus chose His close circle upon whom the church would be built, He chose fishermen, tax-collectors, men of the land.

For those who are "in Christ," work becomes once more what God intended it to be. When we are "in Christ," our daily work ceases to be under the curse and can become our glad service, a means of working together with God in His work.

God dwells not only in temples made with hands. This is a

truth rescued by the Protestant Reformers. During the Middle Ages common work had taken second place to the "holy acts" of the monks and priests. But Martin Luther reminded the people, "A cobbler, a smith, a peasant, whatever he may be . . . all men alike are consecrated bishops and priests. A poor servant-girl may say: I cook the meals, I make up the beds, I dust the room. Who has bidden me do it? My master and my mistress have bid me. Who has given them the right to command me? God has given it them. So it is true that I am serving God in heaven as well as them."[49]

The Reformers rightly emphasized that a Christian can serve God by faithfulness in common daily work, whatever the occupation. But in that truth is also the making of an error, the idea that all that is necessary is to do your job well. That idea, carried to its extreme, permitted the keepers of Auschwitz to incinerate 2 to 4 million Jews during World War II. They did their work well! So, too, the bartender or Las Vegas casino chip-maker can justify his work.

Henry David Thoreau once commented, "It is not enough to be busy; so are the ants. The question is: What are we busy about? Our work can become fulfillment of our vocation, a means of working with God. But it is not always that. What shall my lifework be?

CHOOSING YOUR WORK

Elton Trueblood says in his book, *The Common Ventures of Life,* "It is terrible to waste food when people are hungry, and it is terrible to waste cloth when people are cold, but it is more terrible to waste a life when so much needs doing."

Ours is a very complicated world in which there are more than 20,000 different ways of making a living. Not everyone has this choice. But most of us have some choice in what we shall do.

Approaching a job choice ought to include:[50]

1. *A look at yourself.* What aptitudes and abilities have you? What kind of work interests you? For what do you have a special knack? Aptitude, interest and personality tests, and talking over your interests with a trusted counselor can help. The parable of

the talents suggests that we are to develop and use, not to hide, our abilities.

2. *A look at the job world.* What jobs are available? Where in the world is my skill needed most? In which job can I make the greatest witness and contribution? Sometimes beginning with a summer job or voluntary service project will help us test our interest in a particular kind of work.

3. *Your family plans.* Do you want a home and children? when? after you have completed education for your job? during your schooling? How will you fit it into your job preparation and career?

This decision is even more complicated for girls than for fellows. For when children come, the wife's work becomes that of a full-time homemaker and mother. But often after the youngest child is in school or through school, a mother may find herself without her biggest job and have time on her hands. Since 90 percent of all women marry, most girls may do well to prepare for both marriage and a career. But never underestimate the importance of the career of homemaking. Responsible motherhood is a top priority job, for the roots of the emotional, physical, and spiritual well-being of a person lie in his early years at home.

4. *The will of God.* While studying ourselves, exploring the job world, and fitting family plans into a career, we need to be conscious of God's leading, of being open to His direction. This involves prayer, the counsel of others, and the kind of Bible study that helps us to know Him better so that we may recognize what He wants of us. It is to ask: "Lord, what will you have me to do?"

ON THE JOB

Millions of people go to work every day. Some face the day's work eagerly, thrilled at the possibilities of a new day. Other workers throw their minds into neutral. They go through the routine of their toil, hanging on from coffee break to coffee break, or from payday to payday. What makes the difference?

Ephesians 6:5-9 and Colossians 3:22—4:1 are passages written to "slaves" and "masters" of New Testament times.

They go through the routine of their toil.

1. What do you see here as instruction also to workers today?

2. What attitudes are important?

3. What about those with responsibility for employing or supervising others?

One employer, speaking out of experience with many workers, said, "A worker is not ready for the day's job unless he's been up long enough to have something to eat, go to the bathroom, find out what's going on in the world (radio or newspaper), and have conversation with his Maker (devotions)."

OFF THE JOB

An earlier generation did not learn to play. We are learning to play—but perhaps not always in the most helpful way. Recreation often becomes wreck-reaction.

Beginning with the need for relaxation, the recreation explosion has hit our culture. Every weekend the highways are jammed as people take to the road, to the lakes, rivers, forests, racetracks, ball parks, and amusement centers. More and more family budgets must make room for bowling, theater, TV, skiing, boating, and hundreds of other items of equipment or types of activity.

Nobody will deny the need for leisure time—to do what we enjoy doing. But the pursuit of pleasure can also become the consuming idol that leaves us exhausted in the race to keep up. The Christian will also be Christian in hours of leisure. Creative hobbies, development of a new interest or skill, or time invested in serving needs of others can contribute to a purposeful use of leisure in our lives.

To be a Christian is an around-the-clock vocation, to which the test of Colossians 3:17 applies: *And whatever you do, in word or deed, do everything in the name of the Lord Jesus, giving thanks to God the Father through him.*

AS YOU PREPARE FOR YOUR LIFEWORK

1. List what you would consider the three most important factors the Christian should consider in getting a job, or in choosing a lifework.

2. What part does and should money play in our choice of work? What, if anything, would you consider more important than salary?

3. In choosing a college as part of preparation for one's work and life, what advantages might the Christian youth find in attending his church college? What opportunities will the Christian youth attending a nonchurch-affiliated college or university seek?

4. In what ways does the call to a "church vocation" (minister, missionary, director of Christian education, etc.) come to people? Have you given thought to the possibility that God may want you to consider serving Him through the church in one of these ways?

PRAYER

O God, I thank You for the privilege of being alive, today, in this world. As I think of gifts You have given me, help me to plan and order my life wisely. For I want my life to bring honor to Your name, and benefit to others.   Amen.

47. Reuel Howe, *The Creative Years* (New York: The Seabury Press, 1959), p. 182.

48. Edward Higbee, *Farms and Farmers in an Urban Age* (New York: The Twentieth Century Fund, 1963), p. 9.

49. *Spirit and Truth,* E. P. Dicke, tr. (London: The Lutterworth Press, 1935), p. 171.

50. Adapted from Edith Graber, *Choice* (Newton, Kansas: Faith and Life Press, 1963), pp. 85-88.

Chapter 25

Teach Us to Pray

Have no anxiety about anything, but in everything by prayer and supplication with thanksgiving let your requests be made known to God. Philippians 4:6

HOW CAN I GET CLOSER TO GOD?

Ruth doesn't understand. What's happened? she wonders as she touches the Bible on the bedside table. Her hand hesitates. Why has she lost interest in reading? And praying—it all seems so hollow. Often she skips it altogether.

How different it was just three months ago! Ruth had come home from camp intensely excited. For the first time, silence had meant something. Morning watch was always over too quickly. Oh, at first her mind kept wandering . . . so many things to think about. But in the quiet she found herself also thinking about God . . . and the world, wonderful and frightening, and God's love in Jesus . . . and about her life, her mother and dad, and friends . . . some of her friends had real problems. How glad she was to be loved . . . and to feel part of God's wonderful plan for people, and the world. . . .

Pastor Anderson's campfire talks on prayer made God seem so real. Pastor Anderson was a wonderful person. He made you feel you could talk to him about anything! And you knew he was listening and interested. He must live close to God, thought Ruth.

Pastor Anderson had talked of how every Christian needs to cultivate friendship with God. "If you don't breathe, you die. If you don't pray, you die spiritually," he had said. And Ruth had vowed to herself: "I will. I will read and pray every day!"

196

*Campfire talks on prayer made God seem **real**.*

And at first she had. Every day she prayed for each of her cabin mates, her counselor, her mother and dad, and some of her friends.

But now—why had she started skipping it? What was happening to her? "O God . . . help me. . . . help me to learn to pray," she blurted out.

How can I get closer to God? All the time we make decisions. Big decisions, too. How do I keep alive my commitment to Christ when a world that does not know Christ tries to push me into its mold? With whom will I spend my life? What shall my work be? In facing these, and the many other questions of growing up, we need help. And we want the kind of help and power we see in others, a power that has to come from God.

LEARNING FROM JESUS

A day came for the disciples when they could stand it no longer. So they asked Jesus.

For months now, Jesus had submerged himself in the pressing multitudes of sick, hungry, fearful, searching people. Sometimes the disciples had become tired and impatient when the crowds pressed in so close, for so long. Yet Jesus did not. Always there seemed to be that reserve of energy and power, of love and kindness.

But the disciples had also seen how at the end of the day, or very early in the morning, Jesus went off by himself to pray. Luke tells of that day the disciples came to Jesus, and finally asked: "Lord, teach us to pray."

Jesus replied: *"When you pray, say:*
'Father, hallowed be thy name.
Thy kingdom come.
Give us each day our daily bread;
    and forgive us our sins, for we ourselves forgive every one
    who is indebted to us;
and lead us not into temptation' " (Lk. 11:1-4).

Luke gives us this brief form of the Lord's Prayer. The longer, expanded form, used by the church in its worship is found in Matthew 6:9-13 (King James Version):
Our Father which art in heaven,
Hallowed be thy name.
Thy kingdom come.
Thy will be done in earth, as it is in heaven.
Give us this day our daily bread.
And forgive us our debts, as we forgive our debtors.
And lead us not into temptation, but deliver us from evil:
For thine is the kingdom, and the power, and the glory,
for ever. Amen.

WHAT DOES THE LORD'S PRAYER SAY ABOUT PRAYING?

Many times we have repeated the Lord's Prayer. But Jesus must have meant more than simply for us to repeat these words. What can we learn about praying from Jesus' prayer?

1. Look at the form of address, "Our Father." With whom does

prayer begin? Are *we,* in our need, the starting point? Or is *God* in His creating, and redeeming mercy, and lordship, the starting point?

Ignatius of Loyola, writer of the classic book of meditation, *The Spiritual Exercises,* states man's utter dependence upon God: "I came from God, I belong to God, I return to God."

All people pray, because they are creatures of God. Something terrible happens. A man says, "God help us" or "Jesus Christ." Even these poor, crippled prayers, uttered without thinking of them as prayers at all, are man's impulse to grasp at something, Someone greater than himself. In fact, long before we begin to pray, God has already been acting in and upon us. God is here, already here long before we make our prayer.

2. What do the opening phrases of the Lord's Prayer say about the mood of Christian prayer? In primitive religion, prayer is often man's attempt to appease a god, to win his favor. Fear of that which he does not understand compels him to pray. (A vivid example of this is the story of Ahab, Elijah, and the priests of Baal in 1 Kings 18:20-29. Note the efforts of the priests of Baal to move their god into action!)

In the Bible, however, we find a people who do not pray from a sense of fear. Here are people who pray to a God in whom they have a sure confidence. Note the prayer Psalms:

> *To thee, O Lord, I lift up my soul.*
> *O my God, in thee I trust . . .* (Ps. 25:1, 2).

Or the prayers of the early Christians, like the one recorded in Acts 4:23-31:

> *"Sovereign Lord, who didst make the heaven and the earth and the sea. . . ."*

This sense of confidence and trust in a God to be adored, is at the heart of Christian prayer. To pray, "Thy kingdom come . . ." is to affirm that God's will and plan for the world is best. And so prayer becomes not so much our trying to bring God around to what we want. But it becomes a way of opening our lives to God, to recognize what His will is, and to offer ourselves for His use.

3. What might we ask in prayer? *"Give us . . . our daily bread*

. . . Forgive us our sins . . . Lead us not into temptation . . ."
suggests that prayer covers all of life. Nothing is too small or un-
important, or too tangled, to pray about.

Our present needs (and we have a lot of them!), past sin (who
of us does not need forgiveness when we stand before the purity
of God?), and future temptation (any situation which is a test
of our integrity)—these are all proper concerns for prayer. In
short, anything that enters the horizon of my consciousness is an
appropriate topic to pray about—that new dress I so desperately
need (or want), my date for the evening, the disgust I feel toward
a dominating person, the exam coming up tomorrow. . . .

PRAYING FOR OTHERS

The Lord's Prayer does not say anything about *intercession,*
praying for others. But Christian prayer is more than an individ-
ualistic relationship with God. Praying for others is assumed.

This prayer Jesus gave, which centers on all the needs of our
life, and which has become the prayer of the church at worship,
can also become the prayer we offer for others. We can use it
by putting the name of the person into each clause:

> Our Father, who art in heaven:
> Thy name be hallowed in Richard,
> Thy kingdom come in him,
> Thy will be done in him today, as it is in heaven.
> Give Richard today his daily bread.
> Forgive him his wrongdoing, and
> Teach him to forgive all who do wrong against him today;
> Let him not succumb today to temptation,
> But do Thou deliver him from all evil.[51]

So we can pray for others, not that our will for that person
be done, or that we shall somehow benefit. But we pray that the
other person shall know God and the fulfilling of God's purpose
in his or her life. We can pray this way for Mother and Dad,
sister or brother, our friends, persons with special needs, and those
persons whom we do not always find it easy to appreciate.

Prayer is listening as well as speaking.

When we pray for another in this way, we begin to know, to understand, to appreciate that person as never before. For to pray boldly, "O God, Thy kingdom come in Richard, Thy will be done in Richard," is also to add "Thy will be done in Richard . . . *and in me!*"

WHAT IS PRAYER?

William Inge once received a letter from a lady who said, "I am praying for your death. I have been very successful in two other cases!" But already we have discarded this notion that prayer is a mechanical controlling of events by our words or thoughts directed to God.

Prayer as "speech addressed by man to God," does not take into account God's part in prayer. Note Romans 8:26, 27, and how the Spirit prompts us to pray.

Prayer is not a one-way street. "Friendship with God" would be a better definition. For in prayer God invites us to live with Him. Prayer is God's sharing within men, His will, His power, and His love.

Prayer is not merely words we utter. It is listening as well as speaking, an attitude as well as an act. We may rightly think of prayer as communion with God. On our part this includes:

Adoration—praise of God for who He is

Thanksgiving—grateful devotion for God's gifts to us

Confession—the conscious opening of our life to God
(knowing that we are known by God)

Petition—making our requests known

Intercession—bringing thoughts about others, God, and ourselves together before God.

Prayer then becomes a way of opening our lives to be used by God, a blending of our will with His will. And so prayer becomes a means of mobilizing us for the assignments of our life. We begin to live in prayer to God, not for ourselves, but for all God's people. As Jesus prayed: *For their sake I consecrate myself, that they also may be consecrated in truth* (Jn. 17:19).

BUT I DID PRAY AND NOTHING HAPPENED

No—our prayers do not always come out the way we hope. A little girl who prayed each night was asked if God had given her an answer to what she had asked Him. Her instant reply was, "Yes. He said 'No!' "

And sometimes we may see nothing happening. But it is hardly ever possible to see from the start all that God is accomplishing. Be patient.

But common sense is also needed. To come near to God is to change. We've talked of prayer as raising our desires to God to see if they are agreeable to Him. Sometimes a web of relationships must be untangled before praying will help.

"He who rises from his knees a better man, his prayer has been granted." (William Inge)

MAKE PRAYER A HABIT

God wants you. God wants you to grow. Give yourself time to grow. Make provision in each day for time with God. Here are a few suggestions to help you.

1. Read several verses or a chapter from the Bible each day. Let prayer ideas arise from the passage you read. (Reading through one book at a time may be more helpful than picking verses at random.)

2. Write down concerns for prayer. Pray for specific needs and for people by name.

3. Each day pray for at least one other person.

4. Though you can pray anytime, anywhere, a specific time and place for devotions each day may help you remember to keep your appointment with God.

5. When you hit a dry spell and lose interest, don't be afraid to start over again.

6. Don't forget to thank God.

Here are some prayers to help you get started:

God, I want to give my life to You.

O God, I want to know You better. Help me to obey You more joyfully.

Father in heaven, guide my thoughts.

Give me the capacity and willingness to think deeply, to speak thoughtfully, and to act with kindness.

WHAT DOES PRAYER MEAN IN YOUR LIFE?

1. What can Ruth(in the situation described at the beginning of this session) do to bring new life into her relationship with God? Where do you feel you need to begin to make prayer a greater part of your life?

2. Would you consider these situations appropriate for prayer? Why or why not?

1) No rain for six weeks. The fields are parched. The farmers will surely lose the crops on which their livelihood depends. Pastor Lewis invites this congregation of rural people to return for a special evening prayer service to pray for rain.

2) The speedometer needle hits 95! Sue is terrified. She had no idea this would happen. She only joined the gang for a ride to Junction City in Don's new car. When Archie's gang pulled alongside and challenged Don to "move over or park

it," the race was on! "O God," Sue whispers as her eyes close tightly, "Don't let anything happen to us. Please, don't let anything happen!"

3) Paula takes one final glance in the mirror. One more stroke with the brush. All set. Ed will be at the door in a few minutes. How glad she is to be asked by Ed for the youth banquet. For a moment she thinks: "O God, you must love me to give me friends and wonderful times. Lord, I want You to know that I love You also. And as I go with Ed tonight, help me to be friendly and kind. And Lord, I ask You for the kind of power only You can put in me—power to live up to my love for You—in all I say and do."

3. What do you think?

1) "Maybe one of the reasons we don't pray more than we do is that we don't often tackle jobs that are bigger than we are!"—Eugene Nida

2) "Our circle of concern is as large as our circle of prayer. If we pray only for our family, our children, and Grandpa and Grandma, then it says something about how far our concerns really go."—Leonard Wiebe

51. Charles F. Whiston, *Teach Us to Pray* (Philadelphia: United Church, 1949), p. 125.

Chapter 26

The Christian Views Death

If a man die, shall he live again? Job 14:14.

Jesus said . . . "I am the resurrection and the life; he who believes in me, though he die, yet shall he live, and whoever lives and believes in me shall never die. Do you believe this?" John 11:25, 26

Tense silence. A strange quiet in this car, a moment before so noisy with the laughter and singing of youth. Their team's 3-point victory over Kenton High was great—just great!

But now they're all shook. It was a close one—that car suddenly pulling into their lane. Tires screeched as Paul instinctively hit the brakes, and then swerved onto the shoulder to avoid hitting head-on.

Hearts were still pounding when Paul had brought the car under control and back into the lane of traffic. Suddenly that ball game seemed far away. Every one in that car was thinking of life—and death.

They were thinking about Jeff. Just last week they had all been there—at Jeff's funeral. Jeff—always so strong, and full of life and fun—until that night his car was hit by a train. They had seen Jeff's body, now so lifeless.

They were thinking of themselves. The line between their gay, carefree lives— and death—seemed so narrow, so awfully narrow. For death seemed so final, so terribly final.

DEATH IS REAL

Most of us prefer not to think or talk about death. Death usually claims older people anyway, or other families, but not us. There

Some say, "when you're dead, you're dead."

will be plenty of time to face up to death we usually tell ourselves.

Because death is a mystery we prefer to evade it. Even when we need to face it, we like to soften the blow. We disguise the pain of funerals in flowers and soft music, and the harshness of the grave we cover with grass carpet. Impressive mausoleums and marble vaults assure "perpetual care" for our loved ones.

But death is still the grim reaper, an inescapable fact of life. No illusion, no dream. Death is real and inevitable. Increasing traffic accidents, war, the bomb, and unconquered diseases remind us that death is not exclusively reserved for old age. Sooner or later death comes close to each one of us, in our own life, or to someone close to us. Even youth cannot escape it. What then?

WHAT HAPPENS WHEN I DIE?

There are two common views about our destiny:

1. The death of the body is the end of personality, or
2. Somehow personality can survive death of the body.

There are, and always have been, those who have said flatly, "There is no eternal life. When you're dead you're dead. Period."

The response of people who take this view is often a happy-go-lucky unconcern about life. This was the Epicurean attitude, "Let us eat and drink, for tomorrow we die" (1 Cor. 15:32).

Or again, it leads to an attitude of despair and bitterness toward life. Catch the mood of these words by a humanist philosopher: "Brief and powerless is Man's life; on him and all his race the slow, sure doom falls pitiless and dark. Blind to good and evil, reckless of destruction, omnipotent matter rolls on its restless way; for man condemned today to lose his dearest, tomorrow himself to pass through the gate of darkness. . . ."[52]

But mankind has never been content to believe that cessation of life at death was final. From earliest times people have been concerned about continuation of some kind of life beyond death. Philosophers have spent many hours arguing over what part of the human being hopped off to heaven or hell, and of what this part was made, whether molecules, flux, natural gas, or the breath of God.

HEBREW, GREEK, AND HINDU ANSWERS

The early Hebrew people in Old Testament times believed in a shadowy world under the earth named Sheol. They believed the good and bad alike went to Sheol. Here the dead lived a shadowy and ghostly existence, cut off from man and God. No hope there. Note the Psalm writer's pessimism: *For in death there is no remembrance of thee; in Sheol who can give thee praise?* (Ps. 6:5). Later, though, we find the belief that God can reach even into Sheol, and redeem from Sheol, so that even death could not break the covenant relation to God (Ps. 49:15; Dan. 12:3).

The Hebrews also believed that life continues in the continuity of the family. For the family can remember a man through the years. And sons could perpetuate the name (and therefore the personality) of a man.

To many Greek people, especially those influenced by the Greek school of thought known as Gnosticism, death came as a friend. The Gnostics regarded human flesh as evil. The body was the "prison house of the soul." Death meant the release of the "spirit" or "soul" from an evil body. Now, finally, that which was real, that which was immortal, the spirit of man, could fly away and become part of the great divine spirit of the universe.

Another idea of life beyond death is that of reincarnation. Many Hindus believe that they will be born again, in another shape and form, maybe a dog, a lizard, or a bird. (That explains largely the Hindu reverence for all life, including animal life.) Goodness in this life will be rewarded by a better life in the next. The hope is to eventually escape the cycle of death and rebirth, and to live on as pure spirit.

None of these, however, describes the Christian belief. The Christian looks at death in light of the resurrection. Can we try now to understand the significance of the Christian belief in resurrection?

RESURRECTION, DEATH, AND THE CARE OF GOD

Over a century ago Allen Gardiner was a missionary to the people of Patagonia, a region of South America. His life as a missionary was a record of terrible sufferings and privations. He was found at last lying dead upon the shore beside an upturned boat. And there, where it had fallen from his hands, was his diary, telling of the hardships he had been through, the hunger and thirst, the wounds and the loneliness. But the last sentence, in scarcely legible words, was this: "I am overwhelmed with a sense of the goodness of God."

The Christian faces death with "a sense of the goodness of God." The reality and finality of death are faced squarely. We die. Our bodies decay. But God by the mighty and mysterious act of resurrection recreates us for fellowship with Him. Resurrection is the climaxing act of God's care.

There is nothing here of death coming as a "friend" to release us from an evil body. The whole of our life is important to God! Nor is there anything here of the Greek view of man's soul being immortal, that there is a part of me that automatically lives on and on. The Bible never for a moment allows man to forget he must die.

The Bible writers view death as the terrible consequence of sin (Gen. 2:16, 17; Rom. 6:23; Jas. 1:15; Jn. 8:24). All men sin. All men die. Somehow man's sin and mortality are related.

This makes Jesus' sacrificial death and victory over sin and death so significant. Death is an enemy no longer feared, because Christ entered into the experience of death and was victorious over it! (Rom. 6:7-11; Rev. 1:18).

Christ has been raised. This changes everything! The "resurrection of the body" becomes a way of saying that all that happens on earth concerns God. We are not junked at the point of death. But we believe and trust that God will pick up, fulfill, and complete all our partial, incomplete human efforts.[53]

RESURRECTION—DESCRIBING THE INDESCRIBABLE

First Corinthians 15 is the great resurrection chapter. Here is one of the high points of Christian belief. Here is hope rooted in the victorious living, dying and rising again of Jesus Christ.

After Paul lists some of the resurrection appearances, he speaks of reasons for the resurrection of Christ. In this entire chapter he is arguing for the resurrection of the dead. Not simply a shadowy existence in Sheol, not a flying away of the spirit to blend into a vast impersonal soul of the universe, but the resurrection of the body! But there are no easy answers to questions such as: "How are the dead raised? With what kind of body do they come?" (v. 35).

Paul's best answer is an illustration from nature. He reminds readers that when they sow grain, it must first die if it is to burst forth in new life. A wheat seed has a different body when you plant it than it has when it stands ready to be harvested. The seed dies and is raised in a transformed fashion. What is reaped is different from what is sown, and yet it comes from what is sown.

So, says Paul, regarding the resurrection of the dead, we are sown a physical body, but we are raised a spiritual body (vv. 42-44). What does he mean by a spiritual body? Paul believed: 1) After death individuals will survive. We will be recognizable. 2) To the Christian, the body is also important, because Jesus, the Son of God, had taken on the form of human flesh (Phil. 2:7). 3) Our bodies will be refashioned, remolded by God, and we shall be changed in such a way that we may continue to live in fellowship with God (Phil. 3:20, 21).

Paul admits this is a mystery. But the fact is, in Jesus Christ and because of His resurrection, *"Death is swallowed up in victory!"*

Suddenly Paul comes to a halt. His theological reasoning comes to a climax with a burst of praise and thanksgiving (v. 57). Then he is down to earth with some practical advice. We have a hope in Jesus Christ. With such a glorious hope to look forward to, we have all the more reason to remain strong in faith and active in God's service. For we know that our efforts for the cause of Christ are not in vain.

ARE YOU READY TO DIE?

Many of us will reply, "No." We haven't had time to do all the living yet that we'd like to do. We may fear the experience of dying. Or we may fear the "What then?" These feelings and fears are natural.

Or we may also reply, "Yes, I am ready." By this we don't mean that we *want* to die. We desire life. But the dread fear of death is gone in that "I trust God to be with me in death as He is in life!"

The New Testament claims *eternal life* is God's gift to the believer in Jesus Christ. Perhaps too often we think of eternal life simply as something that happens after death. So we miss the kind of living that helps us to face death.

Stephen Vincent Benét said, "Life is not lost by dying! Life is lost minute by minute, day by dragging day, in all the thousand, small, uncaring ways."

Living is more than simply breathing and existing. Jesus recognized that people are dead on the inside unless they stand in right relation to God and to each other. This was His concern that night Nicodemus came to see Him. He told Nicodemus straight out, "Except a man be born of water and the Spirit, he cannot enter into the kingdom of God" (Jn. 3:5 KJV).

Relationship to God and to man is all-important. Herein lies life of a new quality.

It is the New Testament's claim and the church's belief that in Jesus Christ and only in Jesus Christ can we die unto sin and be made alive unto God. When this reality has occurred in our lives, we can live by the old farmer's saying, "Live as though you would die tonight. Farm as though you would live forever." We are at peace with God. We are ready. Yet we still plan and work as God gives us life.

Does this make sense? A twenty-one-year-old Mennonite Central Committee relief worker in a war area wrote home in reply to questions about his safety. After describing the relative security of the area where he worked, he added: "Security comes also from an inward condition, the degree with which one has come to terms with life, the possibilities of death, and the nature of one's affirmations."

A CHRISTIAN FUNERAL

When Christians gather for a funeral service, they do more than show honor for the person who has died, or sympathy for a family in grief. The deeper meaning of their act is the worship of God. The Christian funeral or memorial service can testify to God's love and power in a time when death and grief seem overwhelming.

But funeral plans are usually made in a hurry, in a day or two. Often this is a time of intense emotional crisis. It is hard to think clearly. Under these circumstances, we are often guided by the customs of society and by what we think people will think. Here are some suggestions that can help us make it a Christian funeral.

1. Call your pastor. His presence in the time of death and grief can be a stabilizing comfort. You will want his counsel and help in planning a meaningful funeral service.

2. Plan for the service in the church. Parents bring little children here for dedication. Young people want to make their marriage vows here. It is here that the congregation gathers weekly

in praise of God and consecration to His will. So Christian people rightly turn to the church as the proper setting for this service of worship at death.

3. Resist firmly the temptation to "honor the dead" by lavish expenditure of money. Expensive caskets, elaborate floral displays, steel or marble vaults are not necessary to show respect. Nor will they make up for lack of love shown to the person in life.

4. Instead of emphasis on the body, focus on the Christian hope! Many Christian people prefer that the casket remain closed at the funeral service.

5. Let the funeral service be an occasion for profound gladness and solemn joy. Great hymns of faith, the reassurance of the Scriptures, the strengthening presence of other Christians who walk with us in this hour, can help us celebrate God's care in life—and death!

WORDS TO REMEMBER

Resurrection. Being made alive again by an act of God. A transforming, or re-creation by God.

Eternal life. Continuing fellowship with God in this life, through death, and after death.

Immortality. Unending, enduring. The Greek view that man has an immortal soul that at death is set free from the confines of an evil body is not the Christian view. But Christians believe that an unending relationship with God, eternal life, is possible because of Jesus Christ.

AS YOU THINK ABOUT DEATH

1. If you discovered that you had just six months to live, what would you do?

2. When you think about death, what do you fear the most?

3. Do you think it is wrong for a Christian to be afraid to die? Why or why not?

4. What hope does the Christian faith give to us? Note Romans 8:28, 35, 37-39.

5. What is the purpose of a funeral service? What elements of our funeral services help to convey the Christian hope and victory through Christ? What funeral customs and practices do you feel are "unchristian"?

A PRAYER

I do want to know You, O God, for I want to live a life that is complete. Show me the dark places in my life that still need the light of Your truth and the cleansing and healing power of Jesus. And make me brave, O God, brave in the hope of the resurrection. For I want to live with You, both now and forever. Amen.

52. Bertrand Russell, *Mysticism and Logic* (New York: Longman, Green and Company, 1918), p. 47.

53. Robert McAffee Brown, *The Bible Speaks to You* (Philadelphia: The Westminster Press, 1955), p. 230.

Chapter 27

Thy Kingdom Come

"I am the Alpha and the Omega, the first and the last, the beginning and the end." Revelation 22:13

". . . he ascended into heaven, and sitteth on the right hand of God the Father Almighty, from thence he shall come to judge the quick and the dead." The Apostle's Creed

THAT DAY!

October 22, 1844! As *That Day* approached, papers published their "last" editions and gave them away free. Men planted no crops, discharged their employees, settled their accounts, gave away their money, and made all preparations for the climactic "midnight cry,"—"Behold, the bridegroom cometh; go ye out to meet him."

On the appointed day they gathered in their churches and waited. When the sun went down on that "tenth day of the seventh month," a date carefully calculated from prophecies in the Books of Daniel and Revelation, they realized something had gone wrong. Christ had not returned! But this disillusioning experience for "Adventists" in scattered New England communities was not the first, nor would it be the last.[54]

Hundreds of specific predictions for Christ's return have been made during the nineteenth and twentieth centuries. The Mormons (Church of Jesus Christ of Latter-Day Saints) went to Utah to await the return of Christ. In the turmoil following the American Civil War the approaching "end of the age" seemed near. So again during World Wars I and II.

214

In 1881 Claus Epp, a Mennonite minister in Russia, came to believe Christ would appear on earth in the year 1889, and the gathering place for the faithful would be somewhere in Middle Asia. He took a group of followers eastward across the Ural Mountains. They encountered unbelievable suffering and hardship. When Christ failed to appear on the appointed day in 1889, Epp discovered he had made a mistake. He had been given his earlier clue, he said, by the dial of an old wall clock whose hands pointed to 89. But now in a vision he had been shown the clock had been leaning, and the end was to come in 1891. Epp was finally cast out by his own group when he claimed to be a son of Christ, and changed the baptismal formula to "Father, Sons, and Holy Ghost."[55]

The Jehovah's Witnesses looked for the consummation of all things in 1914, but later revised this. C. N. Wisner of Richmond, Virginia, expected the end in 1933. He based this on many thirty-third verses of Scripture, verses with thirty-three words, series of words with thirty-three letters, etc. In Chicago, a Church of the Deliverance has a service every Sunday evening from 11 to 12 P.M. The members gather at this unusual hour so they will be found ready when Christ shall come "at midnight" (Mt. 25:1-13).

Such bizarre stories, and the many crude attempts at date-setting, have inclined us not to take very seriously Christ's coming. Yet the New Testament has a clear message that speaks to us of judgment and hope.

SECOND COMING AND THE IDEA OF JUDGMENT

Why will Christ come again? When will it be? What? Why? How? When? These questions all reflect the belief of the early church that Jesus would return as He had ascended (Acts 1:10, 11).

But in trying to understand the second coming, we meet another idea that is basic to it, belief in judgment.

From early Old Testament times God was believed to be the judge (Gen. 18:25). Later the commandments were given to men to guide them in their relationship to God and to each other

215

(Ex. 20:1ff.). Through the years the prophets called the people to return to the righteousness demanded by a holy God. With time, the people came to believe in a great future day of judgment, *the Day of the Lord*. On that day God would punish the wicked peoples of the earth and restore His own people, the true Israel (Dan. 7:21, 22, 27).

THE DAY OF THE LORD—A FIRST CENTURY VIEW

The New Testament writers lived with the belief of a judgment day. For them, Christ now became the judge. They saw in Jesus the *Messiah* who had been promised by God. Jesus had come once to show God's love among men and to warn of His judgment. Now after the resurrection and ascension they knew His presence in the Spirit. But they also expected Him to return at the end of time, as we know it, in the power and glory of God.

At first they expected this might happen during their lifetime. The two letters to the Thessalonians are among the earliest of our New Testament writings. The first letter speaks to questions the people had about the second coming of Christ. For example, what would happen to those who had already died? Paul tells them not to fear or worry, but insists *the day of the Lord* will come suddenly, unexpectedly, "like a thief in the night." He urges an attitude of watchfulness (1 Thess. 4:13—5:6).

When the Thessalonian Christians focused on these words, ignoring the other teachings, leaving their daily tasks, and doing nothing but watching and waiting for Christ's return, Paul wrote the second letter. He reminds them of the signs of Christ's coming, but also that they need to continue work (2 Thess. 2:12; 3:6-13).

The early Christians needed to revise their understanding about the immediacy of Christ's return. Christ's coming may be delayed. But they were sure there would be an end to earthly history, when the deeds of men would be judged. This belief was based on Jesus' parables of judgment as recorded in Matthew 25 and Mark 13. The theme: Watch! Be alert! Be ready!

The Book of Revelation, written toward the end of the first century, is assuring a church under severe persecution that Christ will triumph. Written in highly symbolic language, the Revelation reminds suffering Christians that Christ will overcome evil, and establish His rule over all the world. God will be at the end, even as He was at the beginning!

This note of hope became part of the faith and creed of the Christian church.

LATER THEORIES ABOUT CHRIST'S COMING

The altar wall of the Sistine Chapel in the Vatican at Rome contains Michelangelo's famous painting, *The Last Judgment.* In it the Lord is shown sitting on a throne. Before Him are throngs of persons awaiting the divine judgment as to how they have used their lives on earth and what shall be their everlasting reward or punishment.

Michelangelo's vivid painting reflects the fifteenth and sixteenth century preoccupation with heaven and hell. A popular woodcut, which illustrated many a book of that day, portrayed Christ the Judge sitting upon the rainbow. A lily extends from His right ear. This signifies the redeemed who are being ushered by angels into paradise. From His left ear protrudes a sword, symbolizing the doom of the damned. These the devils drag by the hair from the tombs and cast into the flames of hell![56]

In art and literature, the church of the Middle Ages used these vivid portrayals of hell and the terrors of the last judgment to instill fear into the people.

But then came the "Age of Reason" and enlightenment! Writers in the nineteenth and twentieth centuries began to talk of the second coming in terms of a gradual growth toward perfection in mankind. Some saw the judgment of Christ in the automatic working of history. Gradually, but surely, men would bring in the kingdom of God!

But two world wars, and a cold war spawning "brush-fire wars" all over the world through the twentieth century shattered that kind of thinking.

In reaction, the pessimistic views again gained in popularity. In these times the ideas of "millenialism" and "dispensationalism" flourished. Based particularly on Revelation 20:1-10, and a literal interpretation of Old Testament prophecies regarding the Jews, various theories have been proposed as to exactly where we are in God's scheme of things. But proponents of these theories often failed to recognize the symbolic character of apocalyptic writing like the Books of Daniel and Revelation. Too great emphasis on details we do not know (Mk. 13:32) often gave rise to the confusion described in the early paragraphs of this session. (*Note*: for a description of theories like "millenialism" or "dispensationalism," their source, and how they influenced the Mennonite church, read the article "Chiliasm" in *The Mennonite Encyclopedia,* Vol. I, pp. 557-559.)

GOD STILL COMES!

By now, after such a long detour in tracing ups and downs of this belief, you may well be asking: Well, what about it? Will Christ return in the clouds of glory as the early Christians believed? Or has He already come? Or will it be the slow coming of Jesus' Spirit into individual lives, and so into our common life? Or is this only a "whistling in the dark" when people face rough times?

The Bible was never intended as a blueprint neatly detailing the future. Our attempts to speculate about the future will end in frustration. So we do well to affirm again what we know.

1. *God has come in the birth of Jesus Christ.* A minister was asked by one of his parishioners why he never preached on the second coming. He replied, "Because so many people don't seem to have heard of the first coming!" The Bible's claim is that God has come to us in Jesus Christ. Until we grasp that fact, we are not ready to go on.

2. *God comes in the Holy Spirit.* We need only remember the frightened disciples after Jesus' death, meeting in a closed room. But the promise came true, "You shall receive power when the Holy Spirit has come upon you; and you shall be my witnesses . . ." (Acts 1:8). Witnesses they became, spreading the message of the living Christ through Jerusalem, throughout all Palestine, and to all the world.

Do you remember? I met you. . . .

The power of God, as well as the comforting and guiding presence of God, comes to us in the Holy Spirit.

3. *God comes every day in judgment and mercy.* We are writing the record of our life by the things we think and say and do each day. This is the point of Jesus' parable about the separation of the sheep and the goats (Mt. 25:31-46). *"When did we see thee hungry . . . or thirsty . . . a stranger . . . in prison?"* will be asked by all of us. And Christ will answer: *"As you did it* (or did it not) *to one of the least of these my brethren. . . ."*

"I have seen you before," Christ will say on that day. "I met you during your life on earth. You had an opportunity then of making a decision about me. Do you remember? I met you in that drunk in the street, and you laughed at me. I met you in that new boy enrolled in your school—that dark-skinned boy you called, 'nigger.' Remember? I met you in that old grandmother who longed for someone with whom to visit. I met you in the cry of starving refugees. I have met you before," Christ will say.

We accept Christ or reject Christ daily, in what we do or do not do for our fellowmen. But even as we are being judged every day, the mercy of God reaches out to us. Life and breath are from Him. Forgiveness and hope are from Him. We live by the mercy of God each day.

4. *God comes at the point of death.* That was the theme of the previous session. Death is judgment. For death cuts off the opportunity of making choices regarding our relationship with God (Lk. 16:25, 26).

But death can also mean hope. Many a person has found comfort in the face of death, knowing God is there, too. W. Cosby Bell, a teacher of ministerial students, learned he was about to die in middle life. "Tell the boys," he remarked, "that I've grown surer of God every year of my life, and I've never been so sure as I am right now. I've been preaching and teaching these things all my life, and I'm so interested to find that all we've been believing and hoping is so."

5. *And at the end of history* (in a nuclear age, a live possibility) *we still believe Christ will come.* And there will be judgment—as men flee to the caves and underground shelters! Revelation 6: 14-17 is not at all out of date as a description of the terror "that day" will bring. ". . . and who can stand before it?"

But Christ's presence in "that day" is a message of hope. The Christian can face the future with confidence in the knowledge that God does not forsake His own. The Christian believes the goodness of God is victorious over the wickedness of evil. The God who brings us into being, and who redeems us, will never forsake us. No matter what comes, God is with us! Read Revelation 21:1-8 as a word-picture expressing this hope.

WORDS TO REMEMBER
Eschatology. A Greek word meaning, "the last things," which refers to the end of our life, the end of time, and the truths expressed by second coming and judgment.

Second Coming. The belief that Christ will be at the end of history even as He has been at the beginning, and at the Incarnation. The personal return of Christ in glory will bring to completion His purpose with man.

The Last Judgment. The belief that what happens in human life has lasting consequences.

ESCHATOLOGY AND YOU

1. What practical values can you see in our understanding of Christian eschatology (about "last things")?

2. Are there things in your life you have decided to change because of what you have studied in this chapter? What are they?

3. For additional research: *The Mennonite Encyclopedia* articles on "Chiliasm" (Vol. I, p. 557) and "Eschatology" (Vol. II, p. 246) are helpful accounts of the Mennonite church's understanding of last things in comparison to that of some other church groups.

PRAYER

> Thy death we commemorate;
> Thy resurrection we confess;
> Thy coming we acknowledge—and await.
> O Lord, have mercy upon us.   Amen.

54. Elmer T. Clark, *The Small Sects in America* (New York: Abingdon Press, 1949), p. 36.

55. C. Henry Smith, *The Story of the Mennonites* (Newton, Kansas: Mennonite Publication Office, 1950), pp. 456-462.

56. Roland H. Bainton, *Here I Stand* (New York: The New American Library, 1950), pp. 22, 23.

Chapter 28

The Christian's Hope

It is my eager expectation and hope that I shall not be at all ashamed, but that with full courage now as always Christ will be honored in my body, whether by life or by death. For to me to live is Christ, and to die is gain. Philippians 1:20, 21

QUO VADIS?

As Peter in a cowardly retreat was fleeing the city so intolerant toward Christians, he saw a vision of his Master going straight toward Rome. Falling before Him, Peter inquired, "Quo Vadis, Domine?" (Where are you going, Master?) Jesus replied, "To Rome to be crucified anew."

Upon that, Peter turned back to the city. When condemned to death by crucifixion, he made the request that he be crucified head downward, because he was not worthy to die as had his Lord.[57]

Only a tradition? Perhaps. But the question "Quo Vadis, Domine?" is a pertinent one that every serious Christian must ask. For commitment to Christ and identification with the church of Christ in baptism means that our life is bound up with Christ. Our destiny is to be with our Lord.

When Jesus spoke of being *the way, and the truth, and the life,* . . . could He also have meant that the road to heaven is by way of going through the world with Him!

Where are you going? Are you tempted to wait and look things over? Has your direction been set? Are you on the way? Which way?

Jesus faced the world head-on, conscious of God's purpose for the world, and for His life. His invitation to us is to do the same.

222

The risks are real. The going may be rough. But we can now walk where He has already gone, and with Him at our side.

CHRIST, THE LORD OF HISTORY

Christians believe history is going someplace, for God is in it! The "kingdom of God" is the Bible's term used to express this belief. Christians inherited the term and the idea from the Hebrew people. The basic point of reference for the Hebrews is that great experience of deliverance in the exodus from Egypt.

God must have had a purpose in preserving them, in making of them a nation, and in keeping faith alive during centuries of oppression. Yet "the kingdom," God's reign on earth in the fullness of His power seemed a distant event.

But then, nearly two thousand years ago (according to our way of measuring time) a new message was heard! *"The time is fulfilled, and the kingdom of God is at hand . . ."* Jesus proclaimed. Not in some far-off future is God's reign! But in this very time God is breaking into history to establish His kingdom! He is calling men to repentance so they might recognize the rule of God in their personal lives and in society.

Peter's message at Pentecost echoed this conviction that a new time, a special time, God's time is here (Acts 2:22-24, 32-39).

CHRIST—AND TIME

For us, who think of time as the passing of minutes, hours, days, months, and years, and whose perspective is so limited, all this seems so ancient. What possibly can something that happened nineteen hundred years ago have significance for us now?

But there is another kind of time. The Greek word for it is *kairos*. *Kairos* is time we know not by so many days or years, but by what happens. Last October 24 may have been just another day for you. But if on October 24 you had a birthday, or received a school honor, or ran the driver-training car into a tree, October 24 would not be "just another day"!

What happened in the incarnation, that total event of the life, death, and resurrection of Jesus Christ? Is this an event that merely happened "back there"? Or is it an event that goes beyond mere chronological time? Is this a real *kairos,* God's thrust of himself into human history in a new and decisive way?

Oscar Cullman in his book *Christ and Time,* likens the incarnation to a D-Day in wartime. At the incarnation the decisive battle was fought and victory was assured. But the victory will not be fully declared until a final V-Day when all hostilities are brought to an end.

But the British theologian, John Marsh, in his book *Fulness of Time*, objects to Cullmann's analogy as being too weak. In human warfare the decisive battle may be fought, but the outcome is not yet absolutely certain.

Marsh suggests this analogy. The victory has been won and declared. The incarnation is more like a triumphal procession of victory than only the decisive battle. Consequently, liberation has come. But there may be isolated areas within an occupied country that have been liberated where people have not heard of the liberation and so continue living as if they were under enemy occupation. There are those living in A.D. not yet aware that the battle has been won, that liberty has been declared in a triumphal procession of victory!

The Hebrews celebrate Passover to relive the Exodus as the great act of God's deliverance of His people. Christians see in Christ the climaxing of God's deliverance. This Christ-event has literally changed the world's calendar.

To take the Christian calendar seriously is to recognize time as more than empty duration in which events occur. History is not simply a long list of recorded happenings. But from the perspective of faith the God of Abraham, Isaac, Jacob, and Moses is our God, too. The God and Father of our Lord Jesus Christ is our God, too.

An impatient student challenged his Jewish teacher with these words, "You mean to tell me you believe in those old laws from fifteen hundred years before Christ?" The old rabbi replied. "In the sweep of geologic and biologic time, it was only yesterday that the Jews were delivered." And we can say, "In the sweep of geologic and biologic time, the resurrection of Jesus Christ was only this morning!"

Are these events really so dated? by whose perspective? Every year, this year, now is A.D., Anno Domini, the year of our Lord!

A WORD ABOUT HELL AND HEAVEN

If the incarnation is victory, and in Christ is deliverance, we still face the fact that the kingdom has not yet become a reality in every life. And there is a horrible picture of the destiny that awaits those who never really begin to live, those who never open their hearts to the outpouring of God's love.

The New Testament word most frequently translated "hell," is the Greek word *Gehenna*. *Gehenna* was the name of a deep gorge near Jerusalem. Some 670 feet deep, it became the garbage dump, a place of refuse, litter, and smoldering fires.

It was the word *Gehenna* that became a word picture of the worst that could happen to a man. To be discarded on the garbage dump of the universe, to be separated, cut off, desolate, with no meaning . . . to be separated from God—what could possibly be worse?

Whatever Jesus may have meant in His use of the word *hell,* it is impossible to soften the severity of Jesus' warning against unrepented sin. One can only stand in awe before God the Judge of all, when one reads Jesus' words in Mark 9:43-48; Matthew 13:42, 50; and 24:41. Separation from Christ in life, and in death, is hell. The somber fact is that we can reject God's love and so place ourselves outside the benefits of that love.

But fellowship with Christ is heaven. And the New Testament speaks a lot more about heaven and eternal life than about hell. It takes the action of God to break the powers of evil that hold sway over people's lives. God delivers men from evil by His love shown in Jesus Christ. All who respond to Christ by becoming servants of Christ are in His keeping. Heaven is a continuation of that life with God which we enter in Christ.

Jesus took for granted the possibility of continuing life with God. It is this that gives consistency to His teaching about the sacredness of human personality (Lk. 15:4), the importance of personal relations (Mt. 5:43-45), the call to serve God's purposes (Mt. 9:29), and His death on the cross.

"Let not your hearts be troubled . . . ," Jesus said. *"In my Father's house . . . I go to prepare a place for you* (Jn. 14:1-3). One Christian described a dream she had of heaven. The gates that opened for her were like the doors of the church where she had been a lifelong member. The doorkeeper strikingly resembled the man who had been her pastor for many years. The job to which he assigned her was darning the socks and patching the overalls of the children playing there!

We smile. Nevertheless, the Bible writers describe heaven in terms familiar to them. Jesus spoke of *paradise* (Lk. 23:43). Paul speaks of being *with Christ* or *with the Lord* (Phil. 1:23; 1 Thess. 4:17). The writer of Revelation thinks in terms of a city, a new Jerusalem, where there will be enough food and water, peace and joyous activity, and God. And all which threatens and harasses will be no more (Rev. 7:15-17; 21:1-7).

Best of all, our fellowship with Christ will be complete and unending. As the writer of Revelation summed up this hope for generations to come, *"Hallelujah! For the Lord our God the Almighty reigns. . . ." There shall no more be anything accursed, but the throne of God and of the Lamb shall be in it, and his servants shall worship him; they shall see his face, and his name shall be on their foreheads. And night shall be no more; . . . for the Lord God will be their light, and they shall reign for ever and ever.* Revelation 19:6; 22:3-5

The final word on this has not yet been spoken—in our experience (1 Cor. 2:9; 1 Jn. 3:2). We can only wait and trust. This much we know: separation from Christ is hell. Fellowship with Christ is heaven. This fellowship is open to us now.

CHRIST, THE LORD OF MY LIFE

But we miss the whole point when we make avoiding hell, or getting to heaven, our first concern. Jesus came into the world to be a servant. His invitation to His followers is to be a servant with Him.

Read again the invitation in Mark 8:34-38. In what way is our initial reaction like that of Peter (vv. 31-33)? What will you yet need to give up to become this kind of servant-follower of Christ? What do you think this kind of commitment to Christ can mean for you?

The Christian's hope is not to flee the world. But as it was for Peter, our task is to face the world with our Master. For only here in faithful service to the mission of Christ, do we find what is worthwhile. *For whoever would save his life will lose it; and whoever loses his life for my sake and the gospel's will save it* (Mk. 8:35).

No, few if any of us expect to be crucified on a cross. Yet, crucifixion takes many forms today! Our life will remain useless to Christ unless it is given to Him to work with Him in the world today.

Among the many decisions to be made in youth, none is more crucial than the question of priority—what shall come first. Only one thing can come first. What shall it be? a famous name? money? a good time? or something else?

Jesus' answer is plain, *"But seek first his kingdom and his righteousness, and all these things shall be yours as well"* (Mt. 6:33). Jesus is saying: Set your heart on the kingdom. Give yourself to it with no reservation, and everything else you really need will take care of itself!

If you choose to seek first the kingdom, what can this mean for you at home? Will it affect your attitude and relation to your parents, brothers and sisters? How?

How will seeking the kingdom affect your life at school? Will it make a difference in how you get along with other students? Will it permit a greater freedom in saying No to the crowd? Will school become an even greater opportunity to prepare your life for service in God's kingdom?

227

If you choose to seek first the kingdom. . . .

What will seeking the kingdom mean in choosing a lifework? Will it permit you to dare to use your life in a way that will best utilize your God-given talents?

What will seeking the kingdom mean in the way you use your leisure time? in the way you spend your money? in your appearance to other persons and your encounters with them? in your attitudes toward people of other races? in your decisions about government service?

What will seeking the kingdom mean as you think of the place of the church in your life?

In such an exciting world, can you ignore the primacy of the kingdom? Do you dare to try to live for yourself alone? Or can you believe that God is working in your life, and that God has a purpose for you? Can you believe that God continues at work in the world, and that through Christ you are part of His plan?

Will you commit yourself to try to find out how God can best use your life?

WORDS TO REMEMBER

Kingdom of God. Way of life in which the rule of God as revealed in Jesus Christ is accepted.

Hell. Separation from God.

Heaven. Fellowship with God.

Christian hope. The forward look that Christian faith gives to the believer. Hope is the trust that God is at work now and in everything yet to come.

REFLECTIONS ON OUR STUDY OF CHRISTIAN FAITH

1. In what ways do people live in heaven or hell already in this life?

2. "Eternal life is not in 'knowing' the right answers but in relation to God and to others. Far more important than learning a set of facts is learning to live." How are belief (faith) and living related?

3. *A summary*: God has acted in Christ on behalf of all men. Through repentance and faith we can receive this gift of salvation personally. Through the indwelling Christ we are able to live a life of discipleship and be victorious Christians. We have hope that Christ will yet complete His salvation in us.

4. *An evaluation*:
   a. How has this study of Christian beliefs helped you in understanding the church's faith? Do you feel you missed something?
   b. In a short paragraph try to sum up in your own words what the Christian faith means to you.

A PRAYER:

Grant me strength, O God, to forsake all that would lure me away from You. And give me courage to face the world, and walk in it, with the message of Your redemption and hope. In the strong name of Christ, my Lord. Amen.

57. Acts of Peter XXXV, in M. R. James, *The Apocryphal New Testament* (London: Oxford University Press, 1953), p. 333.